Thai Taxi Talismans

Bangkok from the passenger seat

'It is better to travel well than to arrive'
The Buddha

Thai Taxi Talismans

Bangkok from the passenger seat

Dale Konstanz

RIVER

BOOKS

First published and distributed in 2011 by
River Books Co., Ltd.
396 Maharaj Road, Tatien,
Bangkok 10200
Tel: (66) 2 225 4963, 225 0139, 6221900
Fax: (66) 2 225 3861
Email: order@riverbooksbk.com
www.riverbooksbk.com

A River Books Production.

Editors: Narisa Chakrabongse & Stephen A. Murphy
Production: Paisarn Piemmattawat
Design: Reutairat Nanta, Dale Konstanz & Stephen A. Murphy

ISBN: 978 616 7339 08 5

Front cover: Baht in the Buddha
Rear cover: Glass Buddha, King Rama V Plate, Money Fish,
    Fat Buddha, Money Monk, Emerald Buddha x 3
Frontispiece: Fat Buddha on the Bridge
End paper: Stenciled Taxi Company Logos
Author's photo: Courtesy of Jason Tonio Woerner

Printed and bound in Thailand by Sirivatana Interprint Public Co., Ltd.

CONTENTS

PREFACE

by Kiki Anderson

When Dale Konstanz first moved to Bangkok eight years ago, he immediately found himself taking taxi cabs a lot. In fact, he spent hours on end in them. It became not just a way to get around, but an opportunity to chat with the drivers and practice his Thai.

Bangkok taxis are painted different bright colours on the outside: hot pink, cobalt blue, lime green, and the inevitable New York yellow. But inside, they vary even more. During his daily commutes, Konstanz noticed that each car's interior was decorated quite differently, and he became acquainted with the religious iconography and ornate design that are emblematic of quotidian life in Thailand as he wandered through his new locale. He noticed not just the repeated imagery, like statues of the Buddha and Ganesh on the dashboard and glass-encased amulets hanging from the rearview mirror, but other decorations. All of this ebullient ornamentation intrigued him.

After a couple of years spent riding and observing, he decided he wanted to take pictures of the interiors of Bangkok taxis, and eventually, make a book of it. He mentioned the idea at Project Night, a weekly meeting of a small group of artists and writers where we talked about our work, and I suggested he start a blog. At times he reminds me of this, as if to acknowledge my input. But blogs are like art projects, or writing: it's not the idea of doing them that's so important, but the act of doing them. Konstanz has been blogging about Bangkok taxis for three years now. During this time, he has learned a lot about the myriad deities, monks, and religious and superstitious beliefs of Thailand. But if you read his blog, *Still Life in Moving Vehicles* (www. lifeinmovingvehicle.blogspot.com), you'll discover much more.

His blog, and this book, are a point of entry into Bangkok popular culture. From the solemnly sacred to vapid kitsch, from Chinese to Hindu to Japanese to Isaan, the objects and images drivers put in their cars are testament to the Thai ability to adopt, incorporate, and transform elements from other cultures, adding them to their own heritage, with a gold leaf here and rhinestone-studded lotus there, to make it all one hundred percent Thai.

Konstanz's snapshots feature money cats who wave their paws, bunches of pandan leaves that freshen the air, wise monks who stare out knowingly, and suction cups that repair cracked windshields. In his writing, he muses on the rides and includes information gleaned from research. He does it all with a sense of humour, tackling a vast topic with relaxed, insouciant vigour.

This book is a primer of Thai beliefs and popular design. But it's approachable, and just plain fun to read and look at. Anyone who has spent time in the kingdom once called Siam can tell you that easygoing fun is one of the guiding principles of life here. In this way, Dale Konstanz has adopted a Thai approach to this fascinating subject.

Kiki Anderson is a writer, translator, language teacher, and food and culture enthusiast who has lived in Bangkok. Her writing has appeared in publications such as Modern Painters, Utne Reader, *and* Poets & Writers. *She is also co-author of* Bangkok Essential Guide *with Dale Konstanz.*

An eclectic combination of lucky idols including a Hindu elephant god, a couple of pigs from Chinese astrology, and a waving money cat.

Introduction:

The Art of Thai Taxis

A festive soi in Bangkok.

Opposite: The Incredible Hulk action figure embraces the taxi meter.

Cab Capital

Riding in Thai taxis can be unnerving when drivers wildly swerve in and out of lanes or monotonous if you're stuck in Bangkok's relentless traffic, but fortunately cab drivers here can comfort themselves and their passengers with talismans. The majority of the taxis in this city are filled with statuettes and images of the Buddha, Buddhist monks, and Hindu gods and goddesses, as well as amulets dangling on chains, beribboned flower garlands, magical *yan* drawings by monks, and miscellaneous charms that are supposed to bring luck and prosperity, create a peaceful environment, assure good health and physical strength, as well as provide protection for the car, the driver, and those riding in the cab.

If you happen to be in the passenger seat of a Bangkok cab and study the talismans stuck on the dashboard, pinned to the ceiling, or hung from the rearview mirror, you become aware that you are looking into the world of ordinary Thai people and are witnessing an integral aspect of everyday life here. To examine the contents of the taxis is to gain a better understanding of Thai philosophies and ideologies. On the following pages, the photographs and chapters focus on the various talismans and aesthetics related to Bangkok's taxi culture as a way to gain insight into Thai attitudes and beliefs.

In general, Thais and especially cabbies, tend to be rather superstitious, not to mention religious. Most drivers practice the most prevalent religion in Thailand, Theravada Buddhism, infused with folk beliefs. Spiritual practices often further involve combining aspects from various religions including Hinduism, Taoism, Animism, and even Christianity with Buddhism to create a particular type of spiritual

Three taxis in a row share the street with motorbikes.

A blue sky behind a resin Buddha image in a Bangkok cab.

syncretism. This approach to religion maintains that if one god is good, then several must be better. It's common to see images of the Buddha next to icons of Ganesh, the Hindu elephant-headed deity in the taxis, alongside a picture of a Yin-Yang symbol, for example. Even in cabs where the drivers are Muslim or Christian, you sometimes find unexpected mixtures of religious paraphernalia combined with personal items and random elements from popular culture.

While holy objects are usually located within the confines of spiritual structures, in this scenario, you encounter the sacred artifacts on makeshift dashboard altars in colourful vehicles racing around in an urban sprawl. This is logical in a land of dualities. This is a place where traditional ways of life co-exist with modern conveniences. Here, the locals effortlessly keep their customs alive as the country, and especially Bangkok, concurrently drives forward.

Typical Bangkok traffic.

Talismans add character to Thai cab interiors while simultaneously reflecting the individuality of the drivers. Decorating the insides of cabs with various sacred icons and other trinkets is a creative outlet for the cabbies. It's a way for them to personalise the place where they sometimes spend as much as seventy or eighty hours per week. The cabs are their 'home away from home' and the need to express their beliefs and personalities in otherwise generic spaces is no different from white-collar workers individualising their office cubicles.

Thailand, and particularly Bangkok, is a taxi culture. In the capital city, there are over 100,000 registered automobile cabs alone, even without including those in the form of motorcycles, three-wheeled *tuk tuks*, truck-like *songtaews*, ferries, and longtail boats. There are more taxis here than in New York City, London, and Tokyo combined. Consequently, they're everywhere in Bangkok and you can almost always find one for hire, except during the rainy season when everyone and their drenched cousin are vying for a cab. Bangkok taxis are available twenty-four hours a day as most of them are shared by two drivers that each work a twelve hour shift.

It's easy to get hooked on taking Bangkok cabs. For one thing, the cost is relatively inexpensive compared to many other cities in the world. The starting fare is a mere thirty-five baht, or roughly one US dollar. And after the first few kilometres, the charge is only a couple of baht per additional kilometre. It's not uncommon to go somewhere within the city limits for one hundred baht or less, and anyway, the convenience is worth every *satang*. Never mind the inevitability of encountering a traffic jam or two.

All types of people take Bangkok taxis. Thais from a variety of socio-economic backgrounds use cabs, as well as foreigners, thus creating a type of 'equaliser' among people living here. Even those with less means ride in taxis occasionally, especially when there's a pack of friends or family members who pile into the backseat and split the fare. Bangkok taxis aren't just for the upwardly mobile or for those

A green Islamic medallion with a tassel hangs from a rearview mirror in a Bangkok cab.

Isaan taxi driver with a yellow incantation cloth and Buddha amulet.

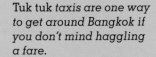

Tuk tuk taxis are one way to get around Bangkok if you don't mind haggling a fare.

with expense accounts like they are in some cities. In Tokyo, for example, a ride from Narita Airport into the city can cost as much as 30,000 Yen, or about 300 US dollars, making this jaunt unaffordable for your average person. In Bangkok, the fare for a ride into the city centre from Suvarnabhumi Airport in a metered cab will run you less than ten US dollars, and that's including the fifty baht surcharge. Granted, the drive is longer in Tokyo, but 300 dollars in a Bangkok taxi would take you to the border of a neighbouring country and back.

For that matter, you can go anywhere in Thailand in a Bangkok cab if the driver is available. Many taxis have charts on the back of the cab's front seats that list all the places in Thailand where the cab will travel including the distances in kilometres and the fares. If you decide to travel this way, don't worry about getting bored during the potentially long ride. Some Thai taxis offer karaoke as a form of entertainment. Drivers that offer this service often have large collections of classic English language pop songs and Thai music with subtitles spelling out the moving lyrics on the screen with Romanised letters.

One of the best reasons to take cabs in Bangkok is to escape the sweltering heat on the streets. Hop in a taxi and you'll immediately feel relief from the scorching sun and sticky air. Bangkok cabbies usually keep the temperature in their taxis comfortably cool, if not downright frigid, especially if drivers notice that new customers have been sweating profusely. And many Bangkok taxi drivers place air-fresheners and herbal scents in the taxi to keep the car smelling fresh, similar to their cabbie counterparts in other cities around the globe.

Picking out a Bangkok taxi to hail is fun as there's a wide spectrum of exterior colours from which to choose. Forget the mundane uniformity of monotone taxis like the trademark yellow cabs of New York City (although we have a fleet of yellow taxis in Bangkok, too). Here taxis range in colour from candy-apple red and flame orange to lime green, cobalt blue, and grape purple. And then there are the hot pink cabs. Where else besides fun-loving Bangkok would the colour pink be used for taxis? London cabbies would turn up their noses at it, but here pink doesn't carry the same associations as it does in the West. It's a colour

Songtaews are a form of transportation available on sois that are especially long.

You can hire a longtail boat to ride in the canals or to any of the piers along the banks of the Chao Phraya River.

A queue of taxicabs in hot colours.

everyone in Thailand seems to fancy, including the King and owners of taxi fleets just the same.

The various colours of the cabs help to differentiate the multiple taxi companies in Bangkok or whether or not they are individually owned. This makes perfect sense in a place where colour plays an important role. Here even the days of the week are assigned different hues. In Bangkok, orange taxis with a white insignia are from Boworn Taxi Company, while the solid green ones are owned by Howa. Purple cabs belong to Laemthong Taxi Cooperative, and companies with fewer than 1,000 cabs such as Nakornchai, own bright blue with red taxis. The two-toned green and yellow ones, on the other hand, are mostly independently owned, although a few taxi companies occasionally use those, too. Many Bangkokians think that the drivers who own their own cabs are the most trustworthy and are the best drivers. But to be honest, I haven't noticed much of a difference between drivers from different companies. There are good and bad taxi drivers regardless of the colour of their cab.

Many drivers have a regular spot for queuing up their taxi. Some park their cabs in front of hotels or near shopping centres, and some line up at the airport. Certain companies have the privilege of working in front of specific locations. Many independent drivers, on the other hand, move around various parts of the city as they are constantly on the lookout for the next customer.

Thai Cabbies

Taking taxis in Bangkok is an opportunity to meet regular Thai people who happen to be taxi drivers. While cabs in some cities have glass dividers between the front and back seats that limit interaction between the driver and the passengers, the interiors of Bangkok cabs are open. Some drivers are very conversational, and you can learn a lot from the cabbies: everything from aspects of Thai culture and lifestyles to major life lessons.

Most conversations in taxis, however, focus on work, family, and significant others. It's not uncommon for drivers to question their customers about their earnings, and it's normal for cabbies to

Opposite: A rainbow of Thai taxi colours.

A colourful custom-made knit cozie for the taxi gearshift.

ask passengers about their marital status. The drivers also like to quiz foreigners about their place of origin and what they're doing here. In other places in the world, a verbal exchange with cab drivers might begin with the weather, but in Bangkok this is rarely a topic of discussion as it's consistently hot. And there's no point in talking about the ever-present road congestion and this city's infamous red traffic lights that can take an eternity to change green.

Bangkok cabbies also like to talk about Thai food. This is a culture where one of the main greetings is 'Have you eaten rice yet?' The local food is a source of pride among people here, including cabbies. They especially love to talk about its balance of flavours and the spiciness. Passengers should be prepared to

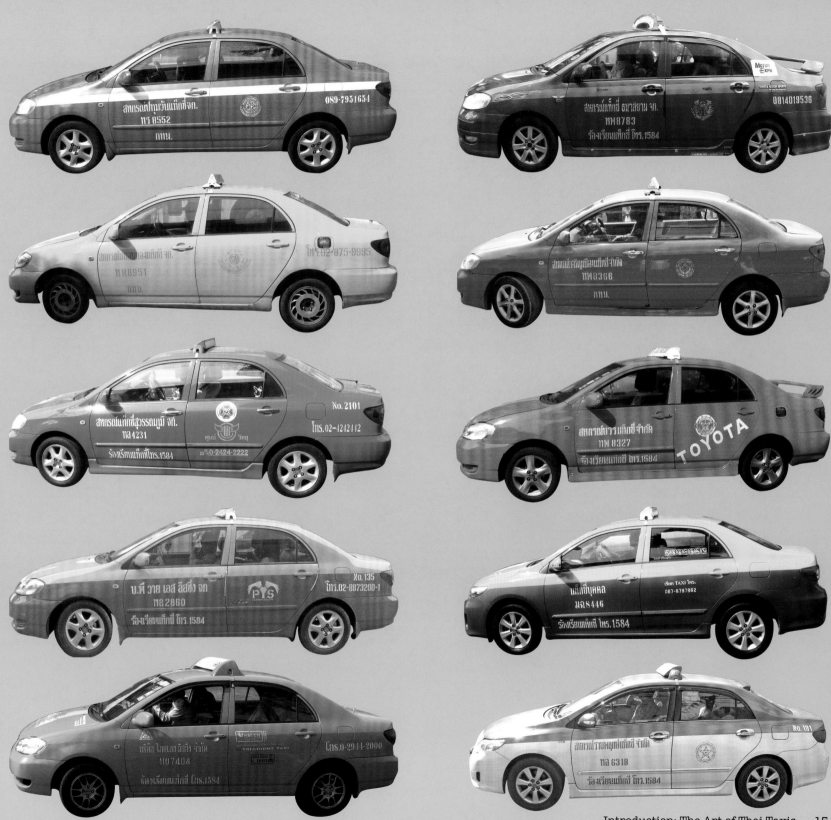

A tariff sheet surrounded by stickers that include a polite Thai kid, an alien, and the rules of the cab.

Right: Karaoke is just one of the extra services available in this taxi.

A lit 'wahng' sign on the dashboard signals potential passengers that the taxi is available for hire.

Right: A TV on the dashboard plays a Chinese period drama.

Friendly cabbie and his red plastic Buddha charm.

This cabbie, originally from Isaan, has enjoyed driving taxis for the past thirty-five years.

discuss their favourite Thai dish with their driver. Tell them that you love to eat extra spicy *somtum* and you'll be guaranteed a huge smile on the face of cabbies from Isaan, the place where this green papaya salad originates and is a staple in the diet.

For foreigners, it helps to be able to speak a bit of Thai in the taxis, as some drivers don't speak much English or other foreign languages except for a few basic words. Yet there are many people here who can't speak Thai who still manage to get around in the cabs. Some drivers pick up some basic English phrases if they work in areas with a higher concentration of foreigners. And occasionally, you meet drivers who can speak English almost fluently because they've worked abroad or they've studied it in school. I met one cabbie that could speak five different languages in addition to Thai, including Japanese, Mandarin, French, German, and English. He loves to talk to foreigners and he also studies the languages in his cab while stuck in traffic and in between picking up passengers. I've even heard about one Bangkok taxi driver who can speak a few phrases in over sixty different languages.

Counting down until the red lights change green.

Southern Thai taxi driver and his plaa tapean lucky fish decoration and Mosque stickers.

Serious Bangkok taxi driver.

If the drivers aren't in the mood to chat, sometimes they crank up the volume on their stereo as a hint to passengers. When foreigners are in the car, the cabbies usually turn the dial of their radio to a station that plays music in English. But usually Thai taxi drivers prefer to listen to *Luk Thung*, a popular form of Thai music where vocalists croon about the everyday hardships of folks from the countryside. Many Bangkok cab drivers also like to play a form of Thai music known as *phleng pheua chiwit*, or 'songs for life' involving social and political commentary. One of the most popular groups in this genre among taxi drivers is Carabao. If you don't believe me, just look for stickers with the band's logo containing buffalo horns on many Bangkok taxi windows.

About fifteen or twenty years ago, Bangkok taxi drivers liked to chat about the stock market. At that time, cabbies were investing in stocks and were quickly becoming experts in trading. Bangkokians often turned to cabbies for advice about buying and selling stocks. Thailand's financial crisis in 1997, however, put an end to the taxi drivers' trust in the market.

Today, many drivers are heavily into politics. A majority of Bangkok cabbies support former Prime Minister Thaksin Shinawatra. His *Ua Arthorn* ('We Care') Taxi Project greatly benefited them and made driving cabs a lucrative career choice for many poor people. The former Prime Minister's reforms allowed taxi drivers to buy their cars at a low cost with low interest. His policies also made it easy and quick for cabbies to get a license. In addition, the initiative enabled drivers that rent their taxis to divide workdays into two shifts with two cabbies in order to cut down the cost of the rental fee. And the project also involved the development of a taxi co-op with its own service centres and group insurance to keep costs down.

Another more recent development that benefits Bangkok cabbies is the use of NGV, or natural gas for vehicles. Introduced to Thailand by the Royal Thai Government, the cost of NGV is almost seventy percent less than traditional gasoline and of course, it's more environmentally friendly. One would think that everyone would convert their vehicles to this type of fossil fuel, but there are fewer NGV filling

Car sign from the 'I love farang [foreigners]' campaign by a local phone company that offers a translation service for English-speaking passengers.

Sticker for Carabao, the favourite musical group of many Thai taxi drivers.

stations in Bangkok than regular pumps making it less convenient to get fuel. And the proper installation of equipment for the use of NGV is expensive. Fortunately, some taxi companies pick up the bill, and other times the drivers rig their engines because they see the benefit and realise that it will save them big money in the long run.

Regardless of these improved conditions, driving a taxi in Bangkok isn't exactly a cushy job. The competition is stiff among drivers as there's an over-abundance of taxis on the road. The overhead is usually high as it includes monthly payments or daily rental fees, registration charges, fuel costs, and other expenses related to car maintenance. Most Bangkok cab drivers work twelve-hour shifts and take few days off, with the exception of a couple of holidays during the year. It also can't be easy driving in a city where some motorists are reckless and treat the centrelines on the road as if they are merely a decorative treatment.

Despite these daily challenges, many of the drivers are easy-going and good-natured. The majority of them are truly concerned about the wellbeing of their clientele. Many cabbies are conscientious about the air temperature for passengers and they often apply decals or car shades to the windows to keep the hot sun out. They also tend to be incredibly patient. Most of them can sit and wait at a stop light for ten minutes without a sigh or a quibble. And they often kindly allow other vehicles to go in front of them. In Thai culture, displays of impatience are considered a character weakness.

Some drivers pride themselves on their appearance. Sometimes they wear neatly pressed shirts with sharp creases on the sleeves, especially when they're donning a company uniform. Other cabbies have perfectly combed or carefully styled hair. Some are even quite dapper and wear a fedora or a fake Swiss watch.

Filling a rigged up tank with NGV requires a special pump.

A sticker reminds passengers to look out for motorcyclists before they open the door.

Two bottles of energy drinks, including *M-150*, tucked between the front seats of a Bangkok cab.

Taxi Trouble

Of course, not all cabbies are reliable in the 'City of Angels'. Some drivers give Bangkok cabbies a bad rap. A fair amount of taxi drivers here look dodgy. Some look like they've worn the same frayed shirt for twenty years, some go barefoot, and others smell like they haven't showered in days. The problem is that the drivers aren't carefully screened, and there are currently minimal requirements for becoming a taxi driver. Almost anyone can get a Bangkok cabbie license. While most major metropolises have stringent exams that require taxi drivers to know their city backwards and forwards, many cabbies in Bangkok have never bothered to look at a map. Some are completely unfamiliar with certain neighbourhoods or destinations. And many drivers new to Bangkok have questionable driving skills, especially those that haven't driven in such heavy traffic before.

Passengers often need to give directions to the cabbies as they are generally expected to know their own way around the city. It's so common to have to explain the route to taxi drivers that some of the first Thai words Bangkok travelers and expats learn are *liew sai*, *liew kwaa*, and *jort thi nee*, or, turn left, turn right, and stop here. For tourists and newbies to Bangkok, it can be perplexing as to how one will ever arrive at the right journey's end.

That's if you can find a taxi that will agree to take you to your destination in the first place. Bangkok cabbies are an independent bunch and some drivers will refuse to give you a ride despite there being a law that prohibits this practice. In some cases, it's the end of the driver's shift, other times they think they won't find any new passengers at the destination, sometimes they don't like the look of potential passengers, and occasionally they're just not in the mood. I guess it's their prerogative in such a laid-back culture, but the

Bangkok traffic can cause a huge headache.

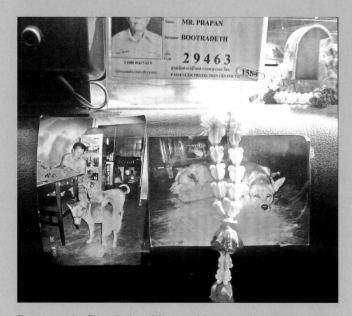

Pictures of a Bangkok cabbie and his two dogs.

experience can be extremely frustrating for those in dire need of a cab.

And then there are those cabbies desperate to make some extra cash. Some drivers take the long way to jack up the fare. Other cabbies get involved in shady practices such as tampering with their meter or recommending and taking passengers to overpriced seafood restaurants, gem shops, tailors, or massage parlours that tempt drivers with gas coupons or a percentage of their proceeds. And some cabbies turn off the meter and offer a rate that's double or triple the normal metered fare, especially in tourist areas.

Some Bangkokians believe that a fair amount of drivers are on methamphetamines or have taken a few too many nips of Mekhong whiskey during their shift. But most of the drivers are merely wired on Thai iced tea, coffee or energy drinks composed of sweet concoctions of sugar, caffeine, taurine, and vitamins. These beverages give cab drivers a temporary boost and the energy drinks are even considered to be medicinal. Almost every taxi in this city has at least one 150ml bottle of energy tucked between the front car seats. In Thailand, there are numerous brands from which to choose, including M-150, Shark, Zone, Lipovatin and the world-famous Red Bull which originates from here, known in Thailand as Krating Daeng.

Background and Stereotypes

The majority of Bangkok cabbies hail from rural Isaan, the poorest region in Thailand. As in other developing countries around the world, the past thirty years have seen a huge migration of country people to the city. Some move here permanently to drive taxis and return home once or twice a year, some stay for extended periods and regularly send money back to their immediate families, and some of these cabbies only drive taxis in between harvests and plantings, or during times when there's no other work to be had.

Drivers from various parts of Thailand often display talismans, objects, and images from their home region in their taxis and it's interesting to hear the variety of accents and listen to cabbies talk about their province. Occasionally, you meet a cabbie originally

Old taxi licenses that never expire.

from Bangkok. Those drivers predictably tend to be the best city drivers, and most of them know the layout of the municipality like the back of their hand.

Most of the cabbies here are men. Out of all the taxis that I've taken in eight years, I've only encountered a few female cabbies. One lady driver told me there are one hundred women cab drivers in Bangkok, but I've yet to see them. I've asked a few male cabbies why there aren't more gals in the business, and the general response was that they don't consider driving cabs to be a safe profession, nor do they think it's an appropriate job for a woman. In a culture where ultra-femininity is a prized characteristic, I guess driving a taxi doesn't fit the Thai stereotype of a demure lassie.

Taxi drivers in this city range in age from barely old enough to drive to ancient. But you can't always tell the age of a driver by their taxi license photo displayed in the cab. Sometimes the pictures are twenty or thirty years old as some drivers have life-long licenses that don't expire. Take a look at the driver and compare their face with their photo on their license, and in some cases, you won't believe the difference in appearance and the way they've aged.

Some Bangkok natives assume that all drivers are poorly educated or naïve. But I've met several drivers who are extremely brainy and some have college educations, such as Mr. Sawat Pholpinyol, who holds a degree in design from a prestigious art school in Bangkok and freelances as a graphic designer. And I spoke to one driver who has a bachelor's in engineering but discovered it wasn't his thing after he graduated from his university and took his first job in the field. In some cases, cabbies have previously worked office jobs, or were involved in sales or retail, but would rather have the independence of driving a taxi. And there are cabbies that are retired or are moonlighting and have another day job. There are even some who drive taxis on their days off from the military or the police force. And one cabbie I met on the weekend is an official driver for Thai Royalty during the week. Regardless of their educational level, many Bangkok taxi drivers are wise. They often possess a wealth of knowledge derived from talking to passengers, reading newspapers and books in their cabs, and listening to radio talk shows.

A rare sight in Thai taxis: a lady driver.

Taxis Past and Present

When taxis were first introduced to Bangkok in the early 1920s, the drivers were World War I veterans. They drove Austins, imported by Phraya 'Phad' Debhasdin, and called them 'mile cars'. In 1926, there were only fourteen of these automobiles in all of Bangkok. Even though the fare was fifteen *satang*, or not even one US Penny per mile, there were other more popular means of public transport at the time, including rickshaws, trams, and horse-drawn carriages. In the 1940s, 'mile car' companies used Renaults and at a reasonable two baht per kilometre, they started to catch on. Later on, Austins were reintroduced in the form of vans, and after that, Bangkok cabbies drove Datsun Bluebirds and Hinos. About thirty years ago, the term 'taxi' finally started to catch on in Bangkok, and twenty years ago, cabs were primarily Toyotas and Mitsubishi Lancers. Today, you see very few other models of taxis on the streets of Bangkok besides Toyota Corolla Altis and an occasional Nissan or Mitsubishi.

Taxi meters are a relatively new addition to Bangkok cabs. In the mid-1990s, some taxi companies started to use meters. Previous to that time, the

Left: An early 1960s postcard shows taxis in front of Bangkok's Wat Saket, or Temple of the Golden Mount.

drivers would roughly calculate the fare according to distance and the transaction would involve haggling a price. Considering that bargaining for purchases is a common practice in Thai markets and in local mom-and-pop shops, it's not surprising that cabs used this approach. Certain types of public transportation in Bangkok such as *tuk tuks* and motorcycle taxis still require passengers to negotiate the fare.

Regardless of the car make or type of taxi, the experience of riding in Thai taxis can be regarded as a metaphor for luck and destiny. Setting out on a journey across the city, passengers have a specific destination in mind, but the drive itself is unpredictable. The chances of encountering a traffic jam are high, and sometimes you may confront roadblocks, police, or car trouble. What will you find inside the taxi? Will the driver be pleasant or rude? Are there any charms on the dashboard that will bring a sense of peace and contentment?

I've come to realise that the taxi ride itself is as important as the final destination, if not more significant. We're all familiar with the cliché that one needs to live in the moment, but many of us don't practice this way of thinking on a regular basis.

A picture of a red taxi in front of Bangkok's Wat Phra Kaew, or Temple of the Emerald Buddha, on a postcard circa 1962.

We're too busy striving to achieve our goals as we try to 'get it all done'. The next time you take a taxi, I recommend that you sit back, take a deep breath, and appreciate the here and now. And if you're riding in a Thai taxi, don't forget to say a prayer to the talismans.

You can choose from a wide variety of lucky charms or religious icons in the cabs as illustrated in the photographs on the pages that follow. Whether it's extra money that you need, love that you're trying to attract, luck that you want to procure, or protection from danger that you're trying to avoid, the talismans in Thai taxis can be of assistance. At least that's what Thai taxi drivers believe.

Collections of little plush characters, toy cars, and feathery hair clips adorn a taxi dashboard.

Bangkok cabbies need heroes such as this Mr. Incredible figure stuck to the rearview mirror.

A Buddha image embossed on a metal plate.

Although the Buddha is said to have asked that no images be made in his honour, followers of his teachings have long paid respect to statues and other representations of him. In Bangkok, images of the Buddha are everywhere: in temples, shrines, homes, schools, businesses, markets, noodle shops, and, naturally, in the taxis.

The Buddha images in cabs take many different forms. Of course, there are often Buddha statuettes placed on the dashboard. But it's also common to see photos of Buddha statues from temples in Thailand and other parts of Asia, printed graphics or photocopied pictures of the Buddha pinned to the ceilings, and stickers of the Buddha on windows. You can even find images of him on limited edition phone cards proudly displayed in some cabs.

One of the most revered Buddha images in Thailand that can also be found in Bangkok taxis is Phra Kaew Morakot. Known in English as the Emerald Buddha, the original sculpture is actually made from jade. The Emerald Buddha has three costumes that are changed at different times of the year according to the Thai seasons, including one for the hot season, another for the rainy months, and a third for the cool time of year. Some Bangkok taxis have a set of three mini Emerald Buddhas that each wear a different outfit.

Small reproductions and photos of the statue known as Phra Buddha Chinnarat are also common in Bangkok cabs. Considered by many Thais to be the most beautiful image of the Buddha, it was created by an elderly man who mysteriously appeared out

Opposite: Sacred Buddha images protected by the Hindu mythological bird-like creature known in Thailand as Khrut, or Garuda elsewhere.

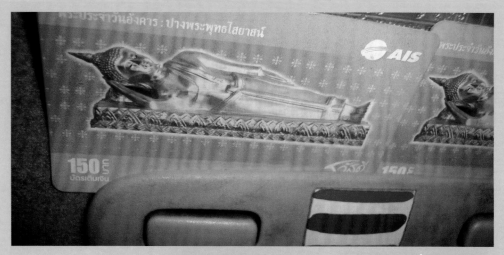

Clockwise from bottom left:

Pictures of venerated Thai Buddhas or monk statues are sometimes placed face-up on dashboards in order to create reflected images on windshields.

Collectible phone cards with the image of a reclining Buddha statue.

Luang Phor Sothorn, one of the most revered Buddha images in Thailand, meditates on top of a re-used orange plastic cap.

A sacred Buddha image encased in a dome.

A yellow glass statuette of the Buddha.

An image of the Buddha on a wooden amulet has supernatural abilities, or saksit, as magical powers are called in Thai.

of nowhere. Surrounded by a golden halo that ends in two mythological serpentine *nagas*, the original sculpture is housed in a temple in Phitsanulok in Northern Thailand.

Bangkok cabbies also favour images of Luang Phor Sothorn because the statue itself is believed to hold miraculous powers. In 1767 AD, the Buddha sculpture escaped the burning capital city of Ayutthaya and was swept downstream to Chachoengsao province, southeast of Bangkok, where it was rescued by locals who tied a string around it and reeled it in. Today, many Bangkok cab drivers make regular pilgrimages to the temple where this image is housed.

The range of colours and materials from which these Buddha images are made is staggering. There are colourful resin and glass statues, or metallic ones with shiny surfaces or coats of aged patina. You can also find ceramic and porcelain representations, jade Chinese-style figures, sandstone versions, and polished rosewood carvings.

Most of the Buddhas in Bangkok taxis are, of course, Thai style, or more generally, Theravada style; Theravada being the school of Buddhism practiced in Thailand, as well as in other Southeast Asian countries such as Laos, Burma, and Cambodia. Getting to know the various styles of the Buddhas can be complicated as the individual characteristics relate to the period and location from which they originate. To exacerbate matters, the styles are sometimes combined or adapted from a variety of influences, and differences can be subtle. The modern Buddha images found in Thai taxis are generally copies of those from six or seven main periods or styles – the Dvaravati, the Khmer/Lopburi, the Lanna, Sukhothai, U-Thong, Ayutthaya and Rattanakosin (Bangkok period).

The Buddha images from the Dvaravati period during the seventh through the eleventh centuries were inspired primarily by Buddhist art in India along with local and Khmer styles. Buddha statues from the Lopburi period, on the other hand, are essentially Khmer in style and have more realistic hair and a slight smile. If you notice Buddha figures

Opposite: A white porcelain version of Luang Phor Sothorn.

Clockwise from left:

An Indian-style Buddha with a Vitarka Mudra hand gesture to symbolise his teachings.

The standing Buddha statue patiently waits for the red light to change.

A Buddha image on a golden medallion dangles from a red cord adorned with jade beads.

with round faces, narrow lips, prominent chests, and stylised locks of hair that look like tiny lotus buds, however, they're probably from the Lanna period of Northern Thailand. Buddha images in the Sukthothai style can be identified by their exceptionally serene and compassionate facial expressions. U-Thong Buddhas created during the twelfth through the fifteenth centuries, on the contrary, are more difficult to distinguish as their traits are derived by combining earlier styles. Lastly, the Ayutthaya style Buddhas are known by their ornate decorative bases and the fact that many are cast in bronze and are large in scale.

A finely crafted relief image of the Buddha.

Another way of looking at Buddha images is to study their hand gestures, or *mudras*. There are six main *mudras*, including meditation, subduing Mara, fearlessness, teaching, and blessing gestures. The meditation *mudra* involves both hands resting in the lap with the palms facing upward and the right hand on top of the left. The subduing Mara position signifies his attainment of enlightenment. Mara represents an evil force that tried to prevent Buddha from reaching enlightenment. In this *mudra*, the Buddha's left hand rests in his lap with his palm upward, while his right hand is curved over the right knee with his fingers slightly touching the ground. The fearless *mudra* consists of one hand raised with the palm facing outward and the fingers pointing upward. In some cases, this gesture is made with both hands. In the teaching gesticulation, the Buddha's hand is held close to the chest with the palm facing outward, the index finger and the thumb creating a circle, and the other fingers pointing upward. Finally, the blessing *mudra* involves the hand extended downward with the palm facing out.

Another way of categorising Buddha images is according to their poses. The postures of Buddha include sitting, reclining, and standing, and several positions are associated with certain days of the week. Bangkok cabbies will often have a Buddha image in their taxi that corresponds to the day they were born. Cabbies born on Tuesday, for example, would have a sleepy reclining Buddha, while those who entered this world on a Friday would have a standing Buddha in deep reflection.

Even if you don't know much about Thai history or Buddhism, it's easy to appreciate the tranquil Buddha images in Bangkok taxis. Riding around this city in cabs, it's also fascinating to see how dashboard Buddhas are affected and often enhanced by the background out the window. A Buddha statuette in front of a blue sky is especially sublime. As you encounter the different Buddha images in the taxis juxtaposed against the moving views outside, you can't help but think that the Buddha is everywhere.

An illuminated Buddha with changing coloured lights that represent the seven chakras, or energy centres, in the body.

A mini version of Phra Buddha Chinnarat, a highly revered golden statue located in Phitsanulok, Thailand.

Right: A Buddha image carved in stone.

Three miniature versions of Bangkok's treasured Emerald Buddha donning different outfits that correspond to the three seasons in Thailand.

Right: This standing Buddha known as Luang Phor Ban Laem is believed to possess supernatural powers and is one of the most sacred images in Thailand. If you were born on a Wednesday evening, this is your lucky Buddha.

Opposite: A translucent glass Buddha statuette alludes to clearing the mind in Buddhist meditation.

A serene still life in a cab composed of a green translucent Buddha image and a Thai monk.

More is More

The attitude and lifestyle in Bangkok calls for more, more, more. Here you'll find a profusion of signage and banners, endless shophouses, malls, and markets overflowing with merchandise, hordes of people crowding walkways, streets jammed with cars, *tuk tuks*, buses, and motorbikes, and rows of vendors on most *sois* hawking everything from noodle soup to cashew nuts.

This is a city of sensory overload. Walk down a typical street and you'll be inundated with smells, including countless culinary aromas, a variety of exotic scents from flowers and incense, as well as a multitude of sickening odours. And then there's the noise pollution. Rattling engines and mufflers on vehicles, piped-in pop music cranked on high, and amplified voices from screaming announcers on the streets and inside shopping centres can be overwhelming and exasperating.

Bangkok taxis are the perfect place to encounter the Thai notion that too much is never enough. Many cabbies love to fill their taxis with all kinds of things they've collected. Some of the older drivers have been accumulating stuff for years, and in some cases, every interior surface and niche has been decorated and filled to the brim. Typical collections obviously include religious icons. But it doesn't end there. Some drivers collect stuffed toy creatures and cartoon characters, manga action figures, hand-blown glass knickknacks, foreign and Thai coins, animal figurines with movable parts, and mementos from celebratory occasions.

In a culture where a majority of the people are highly superstitious, many of the objects in the taxis are related to such beliefs. Thai cabbies often choose some of the items in their taxis according to

Suction cups seal a crack in the windshield of a taxi decorated to the brim with a variety of pictures and charms.

Every nook and cranny is filled with religious and superstitious images and icons, not to mention random stuffed toy animals.

myths and old wives' tales, as well as astrology and numerology. Many of these practices relate to making money, keeping ghosts at bay, finding a mate, and evoking animist spirits and the gods. Everything from tree bark and roots to items in particular colours are employed in accordance with these convictions.

Environments created by some cabbies completely transform the vehicles into shrines or living rooms on wheels. The ceilings of many cabs are encrusted with sacred drawings, incantation cloths, amulets, and pictures. Some taxis feature hand-knit seat covers and accessories, including gearshift cozies and steering wheel covers, that blanket every part of the interior and give the cabs a warm, homey feeling; not something one normally desires in such a balmy climate. Other cabs have TVs on the dashboard or affixed to the sun visor for watching Chinese period dramas or Muay Thai boxing matches.

It's also common to see taxi windows plastered with registration decals, adhesive signs, tinted screens, stickers, and decorative images attached with tape. Stickers are available in most markets and from vendors that roam the streets of Bangkok in large motorised carts, and some of their best customers are

Below: Bangkok taxi windows plastered with colourful stickers and decals. Never mind that the cabbies can barely see out their windows to drive.

A decorative plate commemorating the reign of King Rama V is surrounded by a menagerie of statuettes.

Previous page: Forty-Four talismans on pedestals.

Bangkok taxi ceilings sometimes double as bulletin boards.

The dashboard becomes a colourful altar.

Bangkok cabbies. The stickers range from illustrations of Thai kids offering a friendly '*Sawasdee Krup*' to reminders for passengers to refrain from smoking and breaking wind to logos commemorating sports teams and musicians or bands. Other decals on cab windows are from phone companies, radio stations, and organisations that distribute them for marketing purposes. With all of these things stuck on the car windows, it's perplexing how some cabbies can see out at all when they're driving.

The aesthetic found in Bangkok taxis makes perfect sense if you consider Thai traditional art forms. Artists and artisans in this culture have long had a proclivity toward complex motifs and images. As a result, Thai art and handicrafts are known for their elaborate details and rich patterns, as well as their striking colours. One of the best places to view these elements is in the temples. Thai Buddhist architecture is impressive in the amount and the quality of decoration, including multi-coloured mirrored facades, surfaces inlaid with mother of pearl, hand-painted wall murals, multiple golden Buddha images, and intricately carved teak mouldings.

An eclectic combination of accessories.

Idols in various sizes.

Despite the traditional preference for colourful, patterned, and detailed objects and architectural spaces, some designer hotels, upscale boutiques, and trendy fusion restaurants in Bangkok have opted for streamlined and monotone environments with a minimalist bent. These temples of modernity can be a welcome break from the sensory overload that epitomises the rest of Bangkok. Certainly, these venues have cosmopolitan panache and international flair. But these places aren't very Thai. If you want to see the real Bangkok, hop in a cab and experience the true Thai aesthetic of maximalism.

Many Bangkok taxis have one set of matching shiny round Thai-style pillows behind the back seat, but this cab has four pairs.

Following pages: A mishmash of talismans and bric-a-brac in a Bangkok taxi, including figurines of Chinese and Hindu gods, plastic bunnies, and a bank in the form of a waving cat.

Hand-knit car accessories give a homey feel to Bangkok taxis.

A still life of lucky charms encircled with a phuang malai flower offering.

Images adhered to the taxi ceiling offer protection and prosperity.

Money, Money, Money

Before I arrived in Bangkok, I imagined that Thai culture was more pure and less affected by materialism. I was wrong. Maybe Thais were less acquisitive in the past, but today Bangkok is one of the world's capitals of consumerism. Malls larger than some villages in provincial Thailand can be found in many neighbourhoods. And there are markets all over selling everything you can possibly imagine. Bangkok is also home to Chatuchak, one of the largest outdoor markets in the world; another testament to one of Bangkok's preoccupations.

While some Bangkokians can't seem to get enough stuff to fill their homes and their lives, some hard-working citizens of Bangkok find it difficult to come by some non-essentials or even basic necessities. A few of the underprivileged denizens practice the Buddhist principle of contentment and try to ignore temptations. But others often grow desperate. Some turn to buying lottery tickets, others practice gambling on cock fighting or *muay thai* boxing, and many perform superstitious rituals or purchase talismans.

One of the largest groups who collect lucky charms for the purpose of attracting wealth is, of course, Bangkok taxi drivers. Some of them stockpile enormous collections of icons and superstitious paraphernalia. As a result, you can find examples of every possible method of praying to the money gods and goddesses inside Bangkok cabs.

Thai and foreign coins and a piggy bank represent prosperity.

Opposite: Fish talisman made from folded Thai banknotes.

A one thousand baht bill redesigned with images of lucky Thai monks.

One popular money charm is made from Thai baht folded into the shape of fish. The aquatic talismans are constructed from out-of-circulation notes creased with elaborate accordion pleats to create the body and the fins, while ribbons, beads, sparkly sequins, and plastic googly eyes are applied to give details and additional decorative touches. In Thailand, fish are a symbol of wealth. Food from the sea and inland waterways has long been a staple in the Thai diet, and fishing has been one of the main industries for centuries. In addition, the Thai tradition of displaying lucky charms in modes of transportation originated in boats. Thais have long used talismans to appease and show gratitude to the goddess of water.

Another type of fish fetish used to pray to the money gods is made from woven palm leaves, coated with glossy oil or kerosene-based enamel paint. Traditional Thai-style patterns are then hand-painted on the fish's surface to represent fish scales and abstract markings, in hues varying from dark green and red to metallic colours. Known as *plaa tapean*, the fish are sometimes used in multiples to create mobiles, but in the taxis the cabbies typically hang one individual fish from their rearview mirrors.

Bangkok cabbies also display miniature versions of fish traps in their cabs. The traps look like little elongated hand-woven baskets that hang horizontally and are adorned with decorative accoutrements, including bells. The fish traps symbolically catch the money, and sometimes if you look carefully, there's a banknote that's already been captured inside the trap.

Other talismans in the cabs include pairs of birds, piggy banks, and cats with waving arms that lure in customers and consequently, cold hard cash. Sometimes small bags containing grains of rice,

Buddha image made from torn Thai baht suspended in resin.

the crop that provides a major source of income for many Thais, and other dried morsels such as beans, are set out in taxis in hopes of prosperity. And some drivers think that it's good luck to collect coins and attach them to surfaces in the cabs. There's also a host of gods and goddesses that are associated with wealth. A few years ago, Thais and especially Bangkok cabbies went berserk over the god, Jatukam Ramathep, a Hindu-Buddhist mythological god. The craze apparently started with a rumour that someone wearing a particular kind of Jatukam amulet struck it rich. Suddenly, everyone and their taxi driver was heading south to Nakhon Si Thammarat, the place where they're made, to get one. At one point, the Jatukam amulets were fetching thousands of US dollars, with the monks who made the amulets reaping the greatest financial benefits. Most disturbing, however, is the true story of a woman being trampled at a temple by a mob of greedy believers competing to buy a prized amulet.

A miniature Thai-style fish trap for catching big money.

Lucky fish, including a plaa tapean decoration made from palm leaves (upper left) and fish forms created with folded banknotes.

A tiny replica of a fish trap lures in the loot with its beads, bows, bells, and blooms.

Other monks also get involved in various money-making schemes, despite the fact that they are supposed to reject materialism. In some cabs you can find images of monks on fake paper bank notes. And then there's the money monk, Luang Phor Koon, who is known for bestowing wealth upon his followers. Having raised millions of baht for his temple in Nakhon Ratchasima and for the poor, this monk has droves of admirers. Devotees who visit him are usually blessed by receiving a whack on the head with a stack of bills.

Even the Buddha is not immune to superstitious practices regarding finances. A common version of

Thai Buddha statues is made from clear resin with torn loot suspended inside. If the drivers can't afford this type of Buddha, the alternative is to tear up some baht in an attempt to make their funds multiply.

Some traditional Thai Buddhists feel that it's wrong to use the religion in this way and denounce the act of utilising Buddhist and Hindu images to invoke riches. I can see their point, but I wonder if the people who shun these practices would resort to praying to talismans for extra income if they drove a rented taxi for twelve hours a day, supported their entire family in another province in Thailand, and earned a meagre amount of money.

Above: A black Ganesh amulet surrounded by lucky Thai coins on a steering wheel.

Opposite: Buddha image made from torn Thai baht suspended in resin.

Lucky Charms

Most Thais don't leave their home without at least a few accessories adorning their body. Sometimes it involves making a fashion statement, while other times it's a talisman worn for good luck or protection, or to gain admiration from others. Many Thais, including taxi drivers, don an amulet (or a dozen) dangling from a necklace with images of the Buddha, monks, Hindu gods and goddesses, and other lucky icons. The charms reflect the wearer's personal beliefs, values, and superstitions.

When many Bangkok cabbies begin their shift, they remove their amulets from around their neck and hang them from their rearview mirror while saying a prayer. The talismans thus serve to protect the car, as well as the driver and the passengers. At the end of the day, the cabbies put the amulets back on as they utter another invocation to themselves.

Amulets can also be found standing or lying on the taxi's dashboard, affixed to the cab's ceiling, or mounted to other interior surfaces. Sometimes the amulets are displayed individually and in many cases, the drivers arrange multiple charms into rows or other decorative configurations inside the cabs. You will never see them placed lower than the waist of the driver. Traditional precepts dictate proper methods of handling and displaying the amulets, including the stipulation of placing them in a relatively high position.

Amulets are most often made by senior monks from clay mixed with dried flowers and herbs, seeds, pollen, as well as the ash of burnt sacred text. Other amulets are carved from wood, stone, or ivory while some are cast in resin or metal. There are even etched glass and plastic amulets. And some are embedded with another material such as a crystal or a grain

A cluster of Jatukam Ramathep amulets.

Opposite: A collection of amulets and charms stands proud on a handmade display stand.

Timeworn metallic charms dangle on a chain.

of rice. In order to make a pressed image known as *phra phim*, the monk needs a mould, a recipe, and specific ingredients that hold significance, as well as considerable knowledge of spells, sacred script and magical drawings.

The front of the charms generally contain an iconic relief image, while the back typically includes sacred symbols and writing originating from monks and from ancient texts. They are often encased in gold or metal cases that dangle from chains and cords, as well as

plastic boxes. Some of the holders are quite decorative and elaborate while others are more utilitarian. In other cases, they're displayed without any receptacle whatsoever.

The charms can be rectangular, circular, triangular or oval, as well as a decorative shape of curves and angles, and sometimes they have a rounded or pointed arch at the top. The medallion-type amulets are generally not any larger than seven or eight centimetres in diameter, and most of them are less than

Nang Gwak, the beckoning Thai goddess, lures in customers at night with her gesturing hand.

Necklaces adorned with several amulets hang from the rearview mirror for protection.

a centimetre thick. Some charms are three-dimensional, and there are also cylindrical talisman known as a *takrut* that contain a tiny scroll with sacred text inside. Another type of amulet has a phallic shape. Known in Thai as *palad khik*, they are worn or carried primarily by men to attract a partner, for sexual prowess, and for general luck and protection. Even gun bullets and glass marbles can act as lucky charms, as some believe that these talismans possess protective powers.

Only charms blessed by monks, and in particular senior monks, are believed to bring luck, protect from ghosts or car wrecks, as well as generating peace, love, and cold hard cash. Technically, you're not supposed to buy them yourself because it is considered bad luck. But in case you really want a particular icon and no one is offering to foot the bill, especially for rare amulets that cost a fortune, you can buy it yourself

Amulets artfully arranged on taxi ceilings.

and tell others you're 'renting' it. Bearing in mind that you can't own a god or an idol, it's a good thing they're available for rent.

In Bangkok, there are entire markets devoted to selling amulets. The oldest and largest one is located near Wat Mahathat between Maharat Road and the Chao Phraya River, where you can also find traditional medicine, old books, and secondhand gold teeth. Another popular amulet market is on the grounds of Wat Ratchanada, off the intersection of Mahachai Road and Ratchadamnoen Klang Road across from the Golden Mount. Chatuchak weekend market is another good place to pick up a talisman or two. In each place, you'll find locals crowded around amulets carefully studying them with magnifying glasses.

Based on archaeological evidence, the oldest Thai amulets appeared from the 5th century onwards in Southern and Central Thailand and were a form of votive tablet. It is believed that they were collected as sacred mementos from visits to holy sites. Later, the charms became recognised as a way to ward off evil spirits and misfortune. The amulets have been modified stylistically throughout Thailand's history. Today, there are innumerable types of amulets that are collected and idolised. Many of these talismans have images of the Buddha, monks, and various popular deities, but there are also amulets with images of Thailand's current king and royalty from the past such as King Rama V. And some charms feature mythological creatures or figures from Thai literature and folklore.

Opposite: A collection of monk amulets on a beaded necklace.

Upper right: A charm in the form of a turtle hangs among Buddha images to invoke protection, good health, and longevity.

Left:
An amulet with an image of Luang Por Klaih is believed to bring good luck and prosperity.

A large Jatukam Ramathep amulet displayed in a plastic case.

Phra Pidta, or 'monk with closed eyes', sees no evil in a taxi.

Bangkok taxi drivers often know a lot about the various kinds of amulets. They can usually tell you whether they are intended to protect, bring good fortune, or assist in finding love. Sometimes they know the origin and the age of the talismans, and whether they're a fake version of one that is considered valuable. Cabbies will check to see whether the imprint and the surface pattern on the amulets, as well as the materials from which they're made, are genuine. In some instances, they may tell you their monetary worth. Some cabbies will even put their charms up for sale. One driver told me he sells his 'rented' charms for double the original price he pays, especially when he believes that they are extra lucky.

Mr. Sawat Pholpinyol's taxi license and his collection of amulets.

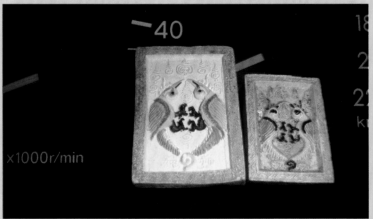

Amulets displayed on dashboards.

A metallic Buddha amulet with jade and amber beads hangs from a rearview mirror.

Long Live the King

Thais love their King and from the amount of decorations that pay tribute to Thai royalty in certain Bangkok taxis, so do some of the cabbies. Decals that read 'Long Live the King' in English or Thai are often plastered across taxi windshields or back windows. And it's common to see banners, flags, and stickers with the King's insignia hung in cab interiors.

Many of the decorations that honour HM King Bhumibol Adulyadej, or King Rama IX as he is sometimes called, are yellow. In Thailand, this particular colour symbolises Monday, the day of the week upon which he was born. Other embellishments, including one version of his royal emblem, include pink because Thai astrologers declared it an auspicious colour for his eightieth birthday. Pink is also associated with the King because a few years ago he wore a pale pink collarless shirt and pink blazer when he checked out of a hospital.

Pictures and amulets with images of the King are also frequently displayed in Bangkok taxis. Because he has reigned since 1946, some of the images go back fifty or sixty years. There are representations that show him when he was ordained as a monk or wearing military regalia, and in some cases he's depicted ascending the throne. In other photos he's portrayed working hard with sweat dripping down his nose or chin or wading through water in rice paddies. Additional images show him surrounded by his admirers, among his family, or with his beloved dogs at his side.

The King's portrait is also on every denomination of the Thai baht, and as a result, many Bangkok cabbies hang up money in their taxis just to look at his picture. The other purpose, of course, is to wish for prosperity. It's also common to see images of

'Long Live the King' decal casts yellow light into the taxi. Outside the cab above the avenue, decorative Thai-style arches include images of Thai royalty.

A laminated collector's card of HM King Rama IX in his military regalia.

A framed picture of HM King Rama V with an image of the Buddha on the ceiling of a Thai taxi.

HM Queen Sirikit and other members of the Royal Family in Bangkok taxis, not to mention in public locations throughout the city and other parts of the country. The Queen is often depicted at the side of the King wearing a military uniform or traditional Thai garments. Some of the pictures of the Royal Family date back to the days when the Princesses and the Crown Prince were quite young. However, images of the highly regarded HRH Princess Maha Chakri Sirindhorn tend to be more recent.

Thais are also extremely fond of King Chulalongkorn, or King Rama V (reign 1868-1910), and his image makes a regular appearance in Bangkok cabs. King Chulalongkorn's image can be found on amulets or statuettes, etched in glass or in fancy frames, and even on stickers. King Rama V is credited with modernising Siam. He helped to reform politics

Pictures of HM King Rama V and HM King Bhumibol Adulyadej with HM Queen Sirikit have been affixed to the taxi's ceiling.

An old photo of the Royal Family in the 1960s and 50 satang coins that contain portraits of King Rama IX attached to the dashboard.

Some of the photos of Thai royalty on taxi ceilings depict formal occasions, such as the picture of HM King Bhumibol and HM Queen Sirikit in royal regalia on the left, while other images are snapshots, such as the picture of the King preparing to perform jazz.

Below: Limited edition banknotes with images of HM King Rama IX and HM King Rama V are collected by many Bangkok taxi drivers.

Opposite Page, clockwise from bottom left:

An image of Prince Chumphon Khet Udomsak known as the 'Father of the Royal Thai Navy' and his father, HM King Chulalongkorn in the background.

A gold medallion with an image of HM King Chulalongkorn, King of Siam from 1868-1910.

A portrait of HM King Taksin sits on a dashboard.

HM King Taksin, once King of Thonburi, leads the way.

A picture of HM King Bhumibol Adulyadej wearing shades (right) when he was ordained into the monkhood.

HM King Rama V depicted on a window sticker.

Below: An historic photographic image of HM King Chulalognkorn stands beside a taxi driver's licence.

A mini portrait of HM King Rama IX waving to his admirers.

Opposite: HM King Rama V's portrait etched onto glass and displayed among statues of monks and the Buddha.

An amulet with an image of HM King Bhumibol Adulyadej surrounded by royal and patriotic stickers

and society, and introduced many new services into the kingdom, including the post, the telegraph, and trains. This king is also recognised for helping the country avoid colonisation through careful negotiations with the English and French. His life is commemorated on 23 October of every year with a special holiday, and Thais, including taxi drivers, regularly pay respect to an equestrian statue of him in front of Ananda Samakhom government reception hall in Bangkok.

Likenesses of King Taksin (reign 1768-1782), and King Naresuan, or Somdet Phra Naresuan Maharat, the King of Siam from 1590-1605, are also occasionally displayed in cabs here. King Taksin and King Naresuan are both revered for their campaigns to free Siam from Burmese occupation. Naresuan's popularity in recent years can also be attributed to a series of Thai films about his life. King Taksin is often depicted in his military garb and you'll know it's King Naresuan when you see his moustache and hair parted down the middle. Both of them are represented in the form of small figurines and in pictures hung on taxi ceilings and occasionally, you even see stickers on cab windows with the likeness of King Naresuan.

Representations of Thai and Siamese Royalty in Bangkok taxis are placed among the gods and other dashboard talismans, showing just how highly they are revered in Thai society. As a passenger in the cabs, one feels distinguished to be among Thailand's esteemed monarchs of today and yesterday. Their familiar faces in the cabs are reassuring as they lead the way through Bangkok's sois and thoroughfares.

TAXI MEDITATION

Sometimes riding in a Bangkok taxi can be a form of meditation. Staring out the window with a seated Buddhist monk talisman on the dashboard leading the way, it's the perfect time to clear out a cluttered brain. If the driver isn't chatty and if the radio isn't blaring, it's an ideal moment to practice deep breathing exercises and to repeat a personal mantra.

It's common to find images of Thai monks in Bangkok cabs. The likenesses are displayed in an attempt to attract luck and wealth and to elude misfortune. Monk talismans are collected and worshipped according to the specific characteristics and magical powers that they are believed to possess.

In the taxis, representations of monks appear in the form of statuettes and small charms, and their images can be found printed as photographs and illustrations, as well as on amulets and even stickers. The monks are usually portrayed in a seated half-lotus or diamond lotus position, or sometimes they are crouched down. Typically, the monks are pictured reading, praying, or meditating. Occasionally, they're depicted riding on the back of a tiger to symbolise authority, or sometimes they're sitting on a turtle to denote seniority and wisdom.

A portrait of Luang Phor Sod, a revered Thai monk who rediscovered Vijja Dhammakaya, a form of meditation that had been forgotten for 500 years.

An image of Luang Phor Thuad peers out from behind a taximeter.

Below: A row of Buddhist monk talismans in front of an encased Buddha amulet.

In general, monks are held in high regard in Thai society. They're affectionately called *Luang Phor*, which means 'Holy Father' in Thai, and they play an important role in this culture. The monks' services are often utilised for special occasions. Monks bless new houses and cars, nine of them are required for traditional wedding ceremonies, and they chant for three days at funerals. Thais show respect for these disciples of Buddhism by giving them daily alms. And in buses and other forms of public transportation, locals give up their front seats for them.

There are numerous monks, both living and long-deceased, who are revered by Thais. However, Bangkok cabbies worship certain monks more than others. Luang Phor Thuad, or Grandfather Thuad, is one of the most highly revered monks because his image is believed to hold protective powers, especially when it comes to thwarting car accidents. Luang Phor Thuad was able to evade dangerous situations throughout his life and some say he lived to be 120 years old as a result. Since his lifetime over 300 years ago, many Thais have believed his image saved them from disasters. One of the most popular Luang Phor Thuad idols is known as the M-16 amulet. This particular talisman is believed to safeguard the believer from gunshot wounds.

Other protective charms include the image of Luang Phor Ngern. There's even one talisman depicting him which is known as the broken gun amulet because it's believed to help wearers dodge bullets. Apparently, some skeptics have even tried to test its bullet-proof capacity by shooting at it directly. According to witnesses, the ammo was mysteriously deflected and some bullets even misfired causing damage to the gun and the hands of those shooting.

A tiny statuette of the Thai monk Luang Phor Ngern nestled in a lined plastic box on a taxi console.

A shiny golden monk statuette in a taxi aligns with the helmeted motorcyclists outside.

Clockwise from bottom left:

A venerated Thai monk, encircled by a plastic flower garland, sits on a blanket of fake fur.

Two golden monk statues meditating on a dashboard at night.

A miniature monk idol on top of the rearview mirror appears deep in thought.

Luang Phor Singh sits proudly on a taxi meter.

Thai monk Luang Phor Koon leads the way in a taxi.

Another popular monk image in Bangkok taxis is that of Phra Somdej Wat Rakang. Also known as Somdej Phra Puttajarn Toh Phrom-rangsri, or Somdej Toh, for short, this monk is remembered for his compassion, patience, and his gift of speech. During his lifetime (1788-1862), Phra Somdej became the preceptor for Prince Mongkut (later King Rama IV) when he was a monk, as well as the abbot of Wat Rakang, or Temple of the Bells in Bangkok. Today, some believe his image is endowed with magical powers,

A healthy yogurt drink is offered to a monk talisman.

A picture of the revered monk Luang Ta Maha Boowa on the ceiling of a taxi.

Opposite: A golden image of Phra Somdej Toh aboard a turtle that represents longevity.

and those who possess Phra Somdej talismans are believed to be blessed with happiness and prosperity.

Luang Phor Sod is another Buddhist monk whose image can regularly be spotted in Bankgok cabs. This particular monk is admired for his devotion to practicing and teaching meditation to others, as well as his rediscovery of the Buddha's Vijja Dhammakaya approach to meditation. Although his life on earth ended over fifty years ago, his teachings still live on today among Buddhists and clearly with Thai taxi drivers, too.

The Thai monk Luang Ta Maha Boonma is also revered among Thais and Bangkok cabbies. Recently, his image has become even more sought-after since he

A statuette of a Thai monk with two decorative ceremonial fans.

passed away on 30 January 2011 at the age of ninety-two. Highly respected for his wisdom, this monk taught his disciples that the best way to honour the Buddha is to practice his teachings in everyday life no matter the circumstances.

For me, the monk idols, regardless of their alleged supernatural abilities, have a peaceful presence and bring a sense of tranquility and harmony to Thai taxis. As a passenger in a Thai cab, if you focus on the positive energy emanating from the monk talismans, you can sometimes avert any unpleasantries that may arise during the ride. And when you arrive at your destination, you will most likely feel reinvigorated and ready to take on the outside world.

A sticker with a picture of Luang Phor Koon on the rear passenger window.

A taxi altar consisting of a duo of monk statuettes, a pair of wooden birds, and an image of the Buddha with red smiley lips.

MONK ART

In Thailand, there's a subset of Buddhist monks who bless businesses and other sites by drawing sacred symbols and script on walls. It's common to see these designs on shop fronts and they regularly appear in various modes of transportation, including taxis. The drawings, known as *yan* in Thai, are often found above the front door of buildings, and in enterprises they're often drawn near or on the signboard. In taxis, most of the creations can be found on the ceiling above the taxi driver's head or front and centre in the cab, but sometimes you can find blessings scrolled on the steering wheel, the dashboard, or even above the car doors.

The designs vary, but are generally made up of white dots, lines and swirls. They're created with a certain type of white powder mixed with water, and at times the monks even draw with black or coloured permanent markers. Sometimes the forms look like towering Buddhist temple structures or like abstract versions of the Buddha's enlightened head. Rows of shapes and symbols often create rhythmic patterns, and sometimes the motifs include symmetrically placed gold squares that add a decorative element. Many of the designs contain ancient script and symbols, as well as Thai writing or even Chinese characters. The text isn't necessarily intended to be understood by the users, but is often known only to those who create the *yan*.

The drawings range in scale from reserved, compact configurations to elaborate patterns that cover the entire surface of the cab's ceiling. And the techniques vary from neatly rendered lines and perfectly formed shapes to thick impastos of powder

Carefully drawn Buddhist symbols and script.

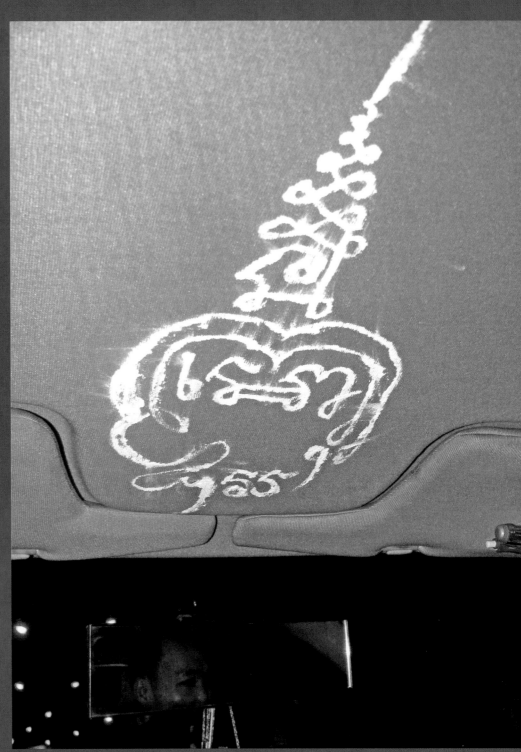

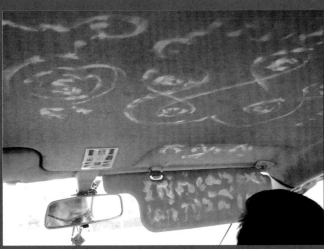

Yan made with holy white powder vary in style.

caked on the ceiling or quick, expressionistic marks and splashes of white. In some instances, they look like careful signatures, but in many cases, the drawings can be elevated to the status of a work of art.

I've asked many cabbies if they know how the Buddhist monks develop their individual styles and approaches to these drawings, but it seems the monks keep their processes a mystery. I often wonder if the monks study different techniques in some sort of monk art school or if they are self-taught. And do the

Monk drawings are often made up of patterns of dots.

monks make preparatory sketches in advance or do they just wing it and draw whatever inspires them at the moment? In any case, the monks are considered to be *ajarn*, or teachers, and their drawings are a way to help guide their disciples.

There's a magical element to these drawings. The symbols and shapes feel powerful, even without knowing the exact meaning of every form, symbol, or line of script. They're intended to bring good luck and fortune, and are created on days and times that the monks consider auspicious. In the taxis, the designs are meant to protect the driver, the passengers, and the car from danger and evil forces. Some of the *yan* have very distinct functions such as shielding the one who possesses it from fire or bullet wounds. And to some degree, the *yan* drawn in the cabs are created in response to the needs of the taxi drivers. If the cabbie

Blessings in Bangkok cabs are sometimes created with permanent markers.

is seeking protection from bad ghosts and spirits, for example, the *ajarn* will create a special design to serve that specific purpose. One taxi driver believes that his *yan* keeps cantankerous customers from acting rude, and another cabbie told me that he hopes that his drawing helps impatient passengers stay calm.

Some disbelievers regard these drawings as old-fashioned and superstitious nonsense. But no one has ever scientifically proven that they don't work either. If they soothe taxi drivers and help them to feel safe, then maybe they serve an important purpose after all. Regardless of whether or not they actually work, the drawings add interest to otherwise bland grey interiors. And spending time staring at these fascinating works of art is a good way to pass the time while stuck in one of Bangkok's infamous traffic jams.

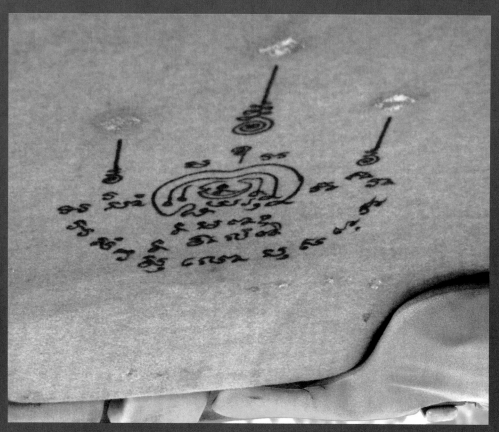

Monk drawings can be found on every part of Bangkok cab interiors including the steering wheel, the glove compartment, and, of course, on the ceiling.

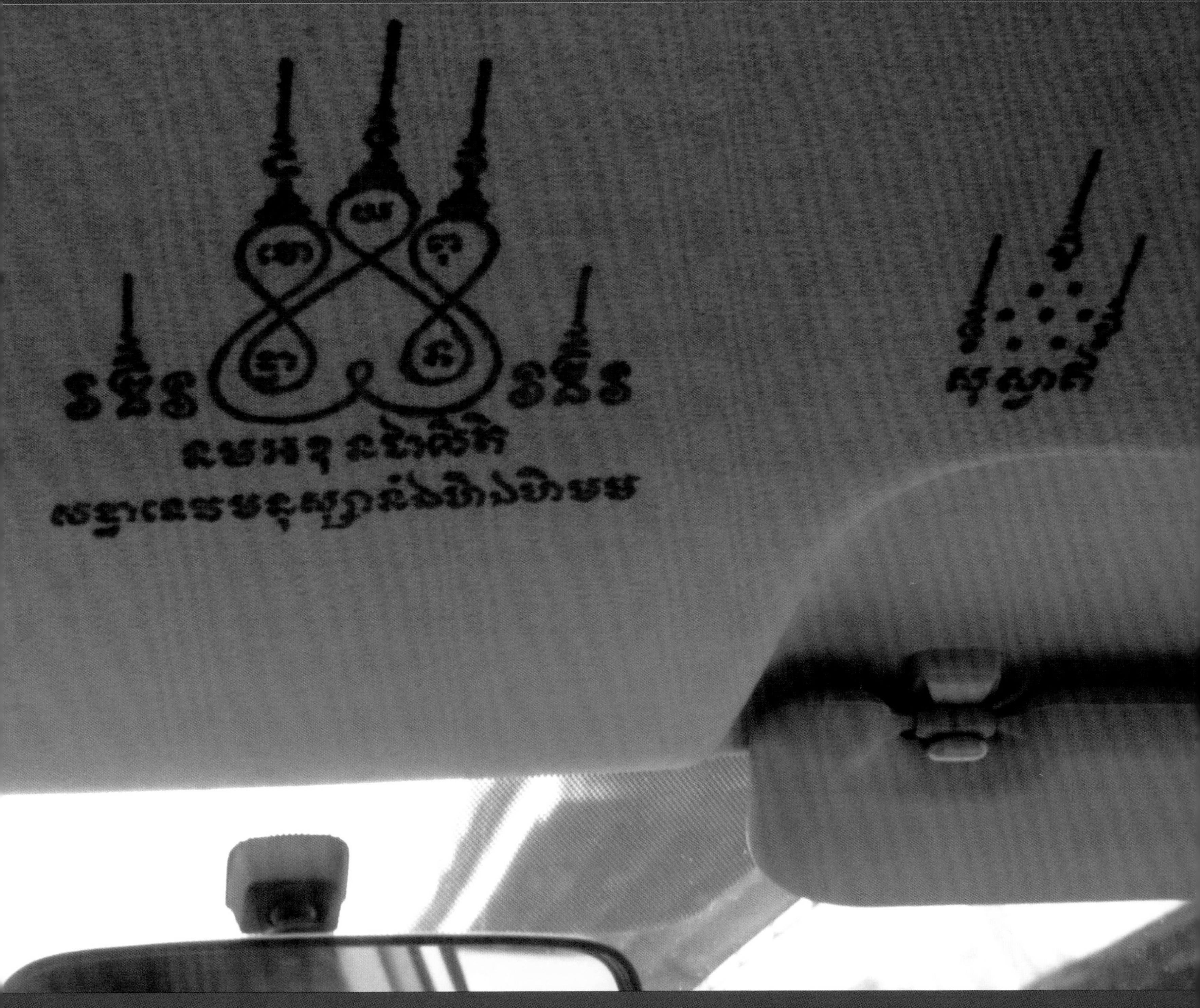

FAT AND HAPPY

It's common to see statues of the 'fat Buddha' on Bangkok taxi dashboards. Despite what some Westerners believe, this rotund and jovial character is not the historical Buddha, Siddhartha Gautama, but rather a figure from Chinese folklore. According to this tradition, this potbellied guy was an eccentric Zen monk who lived around 900 AD. 'Buddha' is a title given to him because he reached enlightenment.

This monk goes by several different monikers, including the name Maitreya which is derived from the ancient Sanskrit word, *maitri*, or from the Pali word, *metta*, which can be translated into 'loving-kindness'. This particular name refers to the popular belief that he is an incarnation of Prince Siddhartha. In Chinese, his nickname means, 'laughing Buddha'. And he's sometimes called Budai, or in Japan, Hotei, which means, 'cloth sack'; a reference to the bag he usually carries.

The linen sack contains all of his personal possessions along with candy for children to denote his kindness and rice plants that symbolise wealth. Overall, the sack represents plenitude and contentment, and as a result the bag is never empty, nor does it ever need to be filled with anything else. He dons a long robe and carries or wears prayer beads to illustrate his religious devotion. And sometimes he holds a golden ingot or is surrounded by coins to illustrate his prosperity. Few would consider him to be a handsome bloke with his bald head, round belly, and short stature. But despite his looks, he maintains a big smile. He is happy, kind, and wise.

A 'happy Buddha' among beads and other lucky charms.

Opposite: A repetition of spheres including pearls, a glass globe, and Budai's belly.

There are many variations of the 'laughing Buddha' image.

In Thailand, there's a similar looking monk figure known as Phra Sangkachai that is displayed in temples, shrines, and of course, in taxis. Phra Sangkachai was an *arhat*, or enlightened being, that lived during the time of Prince Siddhartha. According to legend, he transformed himself into a less-than-attractive chap with a portly physique to avoid being compared to the Buddha who was considered to be a good-looking man with a radiant complexion.

Despite the similar body types of Budai and Phra Sangkachai, there are some differences in the appearances of the two. Phra Sangkachai has a few locks on his head unlike the hair deficient Budai. And Phra Sangkachai wears a Theravadin robe wrapped over one shoulder with one uncovered arm, while Budai wears a Chinese-style cloak that covers both arms, but leaves the chest exposed.

Budai and Phra Sangkachai idols found in Bangkok taxis are made from a variety of materials. Many of the Budai statuettes are ceramic with a less-than-genuine golden finish, although sometimes the images are carved from real jade or made of jade-coloured plastic to reflect Budai's Chinese heritage. Both images can be cast in metal or carved from stone, and sometimes these figures are depicted on amulets or in prints and photographs.

A taxi meter bookended by a pair of fat Buddhas.

Thai cabbies who keep images of Phra Sangkachai and Budai in their taxis rely on them to bring good luck and prosperity. The cheery idols are also supposed to remind the drivers to be happy and content, and remember to be kind to others, especially passengers and those sharing the same road. For cabbies that follow traditional Buddhist principles, the icons are there to prompt them to reflect on enlightenment as the ultimate goal in life.

Many people are familiar with the age-old Chinese tradition of touching the fat Buddha for prosperity and good fortune. I asked one taxi driver who had a Budai statuette in his cab if he ever rubs its belly. The cabbie let out a jolly laugh, and when I looked over at him, I noticed that he looked a lot like his golden statue on the dashboard.

*Mini Phra Sangkachai
images: fat, happy,
and little.*

*Opposite: Budai
communicates happiness
through his big smile.*

THAI ACE COMMUNICATION CO.,

TAXI-RADIO 1681

An offering of rice and other Thai food to various idols, including a rich elephant, a sparkly Buddha in a container, and the rotund Chinese monk, Budai.

Menagerie of Immortals

Nang Gwak cast in metal waves to potential customers.

Many of the divine beings that Thais and Thai cabbies worship are, of course, Buddhist in nature, while others originate from Hinduism as Thais believe that the Hindu Gods protect the Buddha. Shrines to Brahma, or Phra Phrom as he's known in Thailand, are commonplace here, and it's not unusual to find images of other Hindu deities in Bangkok taxis such as Shiva, the creator and destroyer of the universe, Hanuman, the mighty monkey deity, and Garuda, the mythological bird-man, known in Thailand as Khrut.

Many Thais also admire Ganesh, the elephant-headed god. He's a patron of the arts and he bestows wisdom upon his followers. Bangkok cabbies often worship him because he's believed to bring good fortune. This god is also said to be a remover of obstacles, and if you were a taxi driver in this city of traffic jams, road construction, and roving motorcycles, you'd be praying to Ganesh too.

In Thai taxis, images of Ganesh exist in the form of statuettes and amulets, as well as in printed pictures and on stickers. They're made from a range of materials, including metal and clay, and in some cases, Ganesh is colourfully decorated. He usually holds an axe or a goad, a tool used in the handling and training of elephants, and sometimes he's depicted with a rat since rodents can gnaw their way through most obstructions.

Opposite: An elaborate statue of the Hindu god, Ganesh.

A statuette with Phra Narai, the Thai version of Vishnu who destroys evil and bad luck, riding on his mount, Garuda.

Opposite: A statuette of Jatukam Ramathep blesses the taxi, the driver, and the passengers.

Other godly characters and spirits that appear in Thai taxis originate from Thai mythology and folk beliefs. One of the most popular Thai goddesses is Nang Gwak who lures in money with her sticky paw. Her name literally means, 'the beckoning lady' and she's related to the traditional Japanese waving cat, Maneki Neko. You can spot 2-D and 3-D images of Nang Gwak throughout Thailand in noodle shops and on dessert carts in local markets gesturing to potential customers. And of course, you can find her inside Bangkok taxis seducing prospective passengers on the street. Amid other talismans and superstitious icons, she sits Thai style with her legs folded to one side. She may look harmless, but don't forget that it's your money she's after.

Above: Ganesh figures in different styles.

A golden garuda figure (centre) flanked by a tiny monk statuette and a mythological lion figurine known as a singha in Thai.

Opposite: Encased in a dome is a representation of Brahma, known in Thai as Phra Phrom.

Additional figures glorified in the taxis are Chinese and stem from Chinese folk religion, Taoism, Confucianism or Mahayana Buddhism. One of the most popular Chinese characters is Guan Yu, a historical figure who lived during the late Han Dynasty and Three Kingdoms period in China. He's often depicted with a red face, perhaps inspired by Chinese opera where it represents loyalty and righteousness or from Chinese literature, and a long, thick flowing beard. He is sometimes referred to as Emperor Guan or Lord Guan, and is worshiped as an indigenous Chinese deity, a *bodhisattva* in Buddhist tradition and as a guardian in Taoism.

Another deity in Bangkok cabs with Chinese origins is the goddess, Guan Yin. Robed in pure white and sometimes depicted on a lotus flower, she's linked with the spiritual qualities of jade. She's admired for her kindness, mercy, and unconditional love. And she's also associated with vegetarianism, and, in particular, the abstention from eating beef, due to her compassion toward all living creatures. In fact, Guan Yin is actually the femaly equivalent of the male *bodhisattva* Avalokiteshvara, the compassionate 'lord who looks down'. He became widely worshipped in this form in East Asia and, indeed, one of his 33 manifestations includes female traits as described in the *Lotus Sutra*, one of the earliest texts about Avalokiteshvara.

A representation of the Chinese goddess, Guan Yin sitting on a lotus flower.

Golden spirit boy, known as Kumon Thong, is believed to protect and be a moneymaker.

You can never have too many stickers of Hanuman, the monkey god, who originates from the Ramakien, the Thai version of the Indian epic, the Ramayana.

A small picture of Erawan, the mythological elephant with five heads and mount of the god Indra.

A representation of the Thai hermit guru known as Por Gae Ruesi on a taxi dashboard.

The eclectic medleys of various deities on Bangkok taxi dashboards accords with the Thai philosophy that variety is the spice of life. Why limit the possibilities when it comes to worshipping immortals? In this culture it's more logical to have a menagerie of talismans from which to choose. Or if you prefer, you can follow the lead of many Thai taxi drivers and worship each and every one of the gods.

A golden statuette on the dashboard of Cai Shen Ye, the Chinese god of prosperity.

Magical Material

Nang Gwak, the Thai goddess with money stuck to her hand, is printed on a blue incantation cloth.

Attached to many Thai taxi ceilings and hanging in other parts of the cabs are incantation cloths printed with magical charts made up of geometric shapes and lines, mystical symbols, and sacred text. These cryptic diagrams are known as yantras, or simply *yan* in Thai. The word itself is derived from the ancient Sanskrit language and basically means, 'instrument for holding'.

The *yan* function as mechanisms for balancing the mind and for making wishes, and they help to protect the devotee from danger. Bangkok cab drivers believe that the cloths conjure up more customers and help them to avoid car accidents. Yantra have been around for millenia and derive from the tantric traditions of Indian religions. In addition to *yan* printed on fabric, you can find examples on the back of amulets, drawn on paper or engraved on metal, and sometimes they're scrawled directly on various surfaces in Bangkok taxis.

Yan are also created on human skin in the form of tattoos. Known in Thai as *sak yan*, with *sak* meaning 'to tap', the action involved in creating tattoos, the designs are believed to bestow mystical powers, luck, and protection to those who acquire these permanent markings. The tattoos are normally given by a Buddhist monk or Brahmin Priest referred to as *ajarn*, or teacher, but they can also be done by laypeople. Getting these tattoos can be painful as they are traditionally made with sharp bamboo sticks called *mai sak* or alternatively with long metal spikes known as *khem sak*.

Opposite: The Buddha is often depicted on yantra cloths.

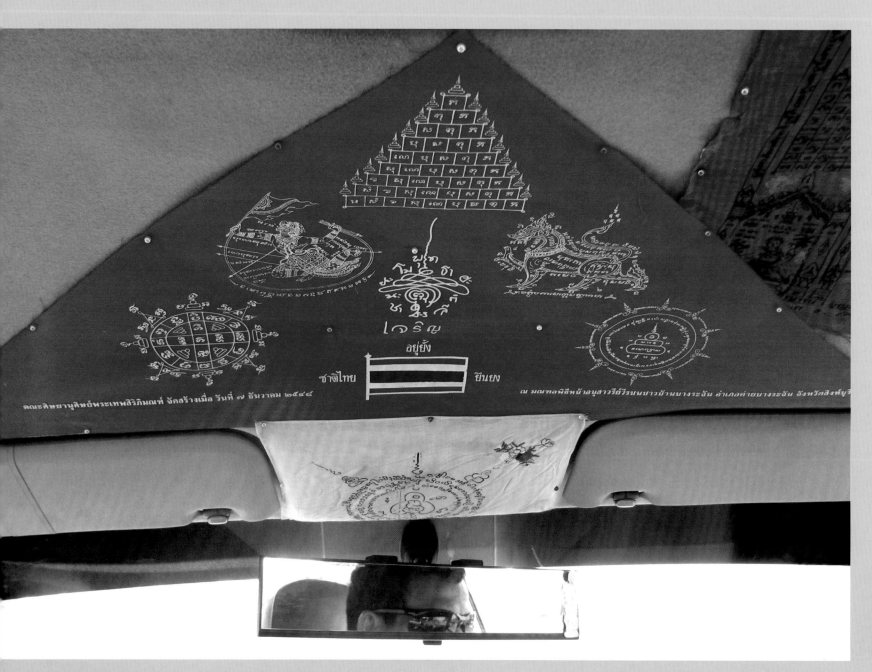

This triangular yantra cloth is both mystical and patriotic.

Many incantation cloths include representations of Buddhist monks.

Each *yan* has its own distinct 'recipe' and combines special magical text and symbols organised in a unique configuration. Thai *yan* typically contain ancient Khmer, Sanskrit, or Pali script, as well as occasional Thai writing or even Chinese characters. In addition, they may have archaic symbols and images of the Buddha, Buddhist monks, Thai or Hindu gods or goddesses, or mythological figures and animals.

A huge incantation cloth on the ceiling of a Bangkok taxi.

An image of Phra Rahu, a Thai deity who eats the sun and moon, can be found on many yantra cloths.

Left: An Indian style Buddha graces this incantation cloth.

Opposite: Red incantation cloths bundled with string and wrapped around dried medicinal herbs.

Every part of the *yan* holds meaning, including each shape, line, emblem, and embellishment. Shapes employed in yantra include squares and circles, with directional line often added as 'the bones of the yantra'. These contrast with stylised organic motifs based on natural forms such as lotus flowers. In the *yan*, circles symbolise the Buddha's face and squares represent earth, water, wind, and fire. Dots, or *bindu*, symbolise the starting point of creation or infinity, stars represent the God Shiva or the Goddess Shakti, and swastikas represent good luck, prosperity, or spiritual mastery.

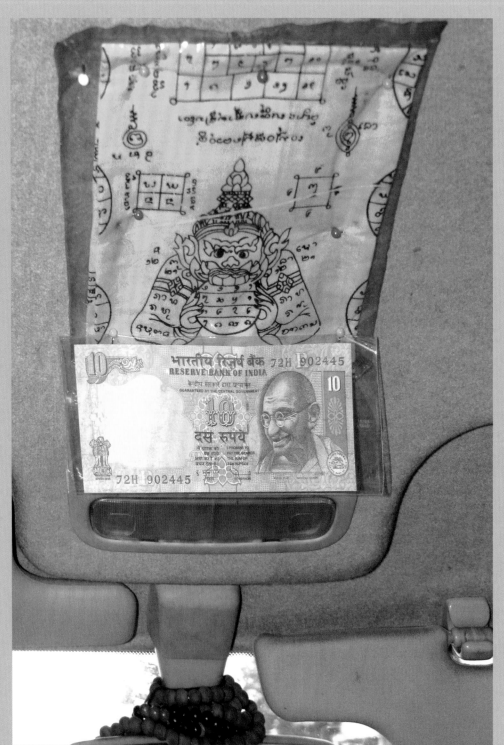

Yantra cloths contain mystical charts and a variety of images, text, and symbols.

A fringed incantation cloth with an image of the Buddha brings contentment to this cabbie.

Yantra cloths made into small sacks with drawstrings contain individual talismans.

Incantation cloths look like small banners or flags. In some cases, they're used to create sacks with drawstrings that hold charms, and other times the printed fabric is wrapped around talismans. The cloths are often approximately the size of a bandana or smaller, but other times they're huge. Those attached to taxi ceilings may cover half or a third of the surface. Most of them are red or yellow, but sometimes you see green, black, blue, or white ones. The cloths are usually made from cotton, but a few look shiny and synthetic. Most of the time their shape is square or rectangular, but occasionally you see a triangular one.

It's not uncommon to see more than one incantation cloth inside a Bangkok taxi. The cabbies believe that possessing several yantras will increase their luck and their odds of avoiding misfortune. The way some Bangkok cabbies drive around this city, perhaps they should wrap their entire car in a giant incantation cloth.

THE FENG SHUI WAY

Many Thais of Chinese descent, including countless Bangkok cabbies, practice the art of Feng Shui, the ancient system of aesthetics believed to yield happiness, peace, and prosperity. The name means 'wind-water', as devotees employ 'the laws of Heaven and Earth' to try and improve their lives. Thai taxi drivers who believe in Feng Shui use it in yet another attempt to deflect evil spirits and to attract Lady Luck.

There are numerous approaches to Feng Shui, including following common sense rules that dictate the arrangement of spatial elements and the placement of worldly possessions. The goal is to improve the conditions that exist between an individual and their environment, and to achieve this, practitioners of Feng Shui believe that it is necessary to alter one's Chi energy, or energy flow, by channeling and re-directing it in one's surroundings. In Thai taxis, cabbies consider how the positioning of talismans best summons customers and cash.

A variety of symbols are used in Feng Shui which are displayed in interiors, including Thai taxis. Representations include creatures from the Chinese zodiac and from Chinese culture, in general. Depending upon the year and the Chinese horoscope sign of the cabbie, you might see images of rats, cows, tigers, rabbits, dragons, snakes, horses, monkeys, chickens, dogs, pigs, and goats in Bangkok cabs. Another common motif in Thai taxis is the round black and white Yin-Yang that represents harmony and balance, as it refers to opposing positive and negative energies. For cab drivers, the symbol reminds them that there will be both good and bad days on the road and that for every difficult passenger, there's one that will be more easy-going.

Feng Shui includes beliefs related to the Chinese horoscope and to auspicious dates and years.

Opposite: A mirrored ball diverts negative energy away from the taxi.

Yin-Yang symbols in Bangkok cabs can often be found in the center of *ba-gua* feng shui energy charts. In Chinese, *ba* means the number eight and *gua* refers to the word 'area' as the map has eight sections in the form of an octagon. It is used to enhance various aspects of life, including wealth, reputation and fame, love and marriage, health and family, creativity and children, knowledge and self-cultivation, career, and helpful people and travel. The maps further relate to the way energy moves within any given space, including the interior of a taxi.

Feng Shui icons are often made from jade, or in some cases, from pale green jade-like resin or plastic. In Chinese culture where Feng Shui originates, jade is admired above all other precious materials, even ivory and gold. It is believed to be a link between the physical and spiritual worlds, and is thought to be the substance that most completely embodies both the yin and yang qualities of Heaven and Earth. As a result, jade is worn and displayed for health and vitality, as well as to ward off bad luck. It is also believed that jade elevates and purifies one's thoughts, and that it helps induce a state of contemplation. Carved or moulded jade or faux jade figures are common in Thai taxis and include images of gods, such as Guan Yin, 'the Jade Goddess', or symbolic animals, including birds, fish, turtles, or '*fu* dogs', as well as folkloric dragons or phoenixes.

Another Chinese mythical beast found in some Bangkok taxis is Pi Xie or Pi Yao which has a lion-dog face. Known as the ninth son of the heavenly dragon, Pi Xie generates good feng shui and has the ability to drive away evil and bring good luck. Considered to be obedient in nature, he also protects his master with his own life. And if that's not enough, he is a wealth enhancer which is perhaps the main reason why so many Thai taxi drivers have a liking for this creature.

Right: A ring of jade represents the heavens.

Opposite: A jade-like version of the Chinese laughing Buddha.

Hanging among other amulets is a yin-yang symbol in the centre of an eight-sided ba-gua feng shui chart which represents the major areas of one's life, including prosperity, fame, relationships, family, health, creativity, career and knowledge.

A trinket with a decorative golden ingot and shiny peanuts are hung in the taxi to generate wealth.

A happy pig from the Chinese horoscope with a faux jade 'fat Buddha' in the background.

Some Bangkok Taxi drivers find inspiration from traditional Chinese proverbs.

Three feng shui wisemen known as *Fuk Luk Sau* are believed to bestow prosperity, authority, and longevity upon their admirers.

A lucky charm in the form of a hybrid creature known as Pi Xie hangs from a rear view mirror in an attempt to eliminate bad luck and attract wealth.

A tasseled silk Chinese lantern charm traditionally symbolises hope, rejuvenation, and celebration.

Other Chinese figures found in Thai taxis include Fuk Luk Sau, a trio of wise-looking deities. Together the three of them denote the attributes of a good life and are believed to bestow kindness on worthy individuals. Each one of the gods is associated with specific endeavours. Fuk stands for happiness as the result of being lucky and is sometimes depicted with a small child to bring further luck to descendents, Sau represents good health and longevity and carries a peach and a walking stick, and Luk stands in the centre holding a gold ingot to symbolise wealth and power.

Mirrors are also commonly used in Feng Shui and sometimes Bangkok taxi drivers hang mirrored balls from their rearview mirrors. Despite the fact that the sphere covered in pieces of mirror looks like a disco ball, their function doesn't involve turning to the rhythm of the music on the taxi radio. Rather, the mirrored balls are believed to avert negative energy known in Chinese as *shar chi* and bring you back into alignment with harmony. In cabs, the mirrors deflect diabolical forces that cause accidents and are believed to reflect natural elements, such as badly needed fresh air, back into the car. They're also used in taxis to counter the pushing down effect of the car ceiling.

Thai taxi drivers who practice the art of Feng Shui often seem well-balanced, grounded, and even-tempered. And when cabbies appear this way, it benefits the passengers, as well. Who doesn't prefer a taxi driver that remains calm and patient during the ride? If following ancient Chinese precepts helps cabbies to feel aligned with the universe, then every taxi driver should decorate their cabs with yin-yang symbols, jade trinkets, mirrors, as well as creatures and deities with Chinese origins.

Placard with a stylised lion and yin-yang symbol helps the driver to maintain mental balance as well as protect the cab from rear-end collisions.

TAXI FLORA

Flowers and greenery are commonly found inside Thai taxis. They add life to the otherwise bleak and sometimes dank interiors, and they help to impart a tropical Southeast Asian feel. Strings of jasmine, along with bright yellow marigolds, red roses, purple orchids, and fresh pandan leaves also make the cabs smell nice.

Some taxis also have miniature versions of *bai sri*, a type of traditional Thai flower arrangement. *Bai sri* are cone-shaped and are made out of real or artificial banana leaves and a slice of the trunk for the base, as well as various flowers that have symbolic meaning. They're usually placed on silver and gold offering trays with pedestals, and are found in pairs. *Bai sri* and other flowers function as offerings to the Buddha, Hindu gods and goddesses, and other deities. They're also a way to make wishes and show gratitude. In the taxis, the drivers use the flower offerings to bless their vehicles, pray for good business, and express appreciation for their job, their family, and for their life.

Many of the blossoms in Bangkok taxis have been strung into flower garlands, known as *phuang malai* in Thai. They range from a simple loop of jasmine ending in a rosebud or marigold to elaborate creations of multi-coloured flowers forming diamond-shaped traditional Thai-style motifs. Some are solely made up of bright marigolds, making them look especially Indian or Hindu in style. Their lengths vary from short ones that tightly encircle a small statuette on the dashboard to long ones that hang down low from the rearview mirror.

These flower garlands are readily available throughout Bangkok. You can buy them on most streets and *sois* and in the markets. You can even get

There are many variations of phuang malai flower offerings, but most of them contain roses, jasmine, and/or marigolds.

Yellow marigolds and magenta orchids dangle at the ends of this flower offering.

A phuang malai seller offers blooms to drivers passing by.

Fresh white jasmine makes Bangkok taxis smell nice.

Thais love a rainbow of colour as illustrated by this colourful plastic phuang malai.

A plastic flower offering in saturated colours creates a cheery ambiance during the rainy season.

them from hawkers who approach cars with garlands that are sometimes strung on long bamboo rods or pipes. After buying a flower offering, the cabbies say a prayer and make a blessing as they hang or lay the festoon of fresh flowers in the front of their cab. When drivers buy flowers from peddlers on the road, the vendors take the old *phuang malai* and dispose of it for the cabbies. Not bad service for 10 or 20 baht.

The *phuang malai* sellers meticulously string each flower bud by hand on strands of heavy-duty thread,

which are then affixed to colourful gift-wrap ribbons cut with pinking shears. The hawkers often wake up before dawn to prepare the strands of flowers for the rush of buyers going to the temples or for those making offerings at their businesses and homes in the early morning. A majority of these flowers come from Bangkok's famous flower market on the banks of the Chao Phraya River, one of the largest in the world where millions of blooms are sold every day.

A festoon of marigolds encircle a Buddha statuette.

Pandan leaves give Thai taxis a distinct fresh herbal scent.

Some drivers display sacred pods in their cabs.

Fresh flower garlands are readily available on the streets of Bangkok.

Silk flowers, like these bright pink ones, are sometimes substituted for real blooms in Bangkok taxis.

A miniature version of bai sri, a type of traditional Thai flower offering.

But not all of the *phuang malai* are made of fresh flowers. Some of them are plastic or silk. Most of these look so fake that no one would ever mistake them for real fresh flowers. This is especially true when the colours are hyper-saturated, when they're covered in dust, or when they've been left to fade in the sun for too long. I'm guessing most of the drivers don't care about whether or not their artificial flowers pass for real. They're probably more concerned about not having to buy new flower offerings all the time. And they undoubtedly save a fair amount of baht by using the same one for years.

If you buy your own fresh *phuang malai*, you should avoid taking a sniff before you give them as an offering as the scent is reserved for the receiver, including the Buddha and the gods. Then again, if you buy a fake one, you don't have to worry about fragrance anyway.

Above left: A not-so-fresh phuang malai *hangs from a rearview mirror.*

In Thailand, heart-shaped or rounded Bodhi leaves are considered to be good luck charms and are often displayed in Bangkok taxis. For Buddhists and Thai cab drivers alike, the leaves bring to mind the sacred Bodhi tree, the type of tree under which the Buddha purportedly sat as he achieved enlightenment around 2,500 years ago. Legend says he meditated under the tree for forty-nine days until he reached this level of awareness.

The Bodhi tree, or Bo tree, is a type of fig tree known in Sanskrit as the *bodhivrksa*, and by botanists as *Ficus religiosa*. The trees, and sometimes clippings from the original, are planted in temples and monasteries in places where Buddhism prevails, including Thailand. The Buddha's tree was destroyed in the 7th century, but another one was later replanted in its place using a shoot from a descendent of the original Bodhi tree that had been taken to Sri Lanka in the 3rd century BC. Today, this tree still flourishes at a temple in India, and its location is one of the four most holy pilgrimage sites for Buddhists.

In early Buddhist art when the image of the Buddha was deemed inappropriate, depictions of the Bodhi tree were sometimes used to represent him. Still today, Bo trees in Thailand are wrapped in colourful cloth to denote their sacredness. The shape of the leaves are also utilised on Thai amulets and in decorations that embellish interiors, including those in taxis.

Golden sacred text and symbols adorn the back of most paper Bodhi leaves.

An image of the highly revered *Phra Buddha Chinnarat* adorns a decorative Bodhi leaf.

Bodhi leaf decorations can often be found among other Buddhist icons and offerings in Bangkok taxis.

Bodhi leaf with a triad of holy monks, from left to right, Luang Phor Chorb, Luang Phor Ngern and Luang Por Dod.

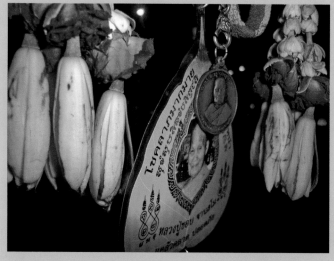

Many paper Bodhi leaves are blue as the colour represents devotion, faith, purity and peace in Buddhism.

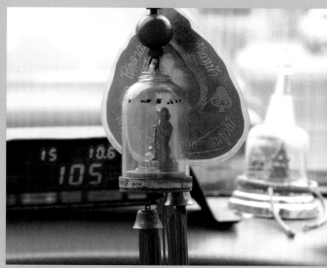

A blue Bodhi leaf symbol with shiny gold script and Thai motifs.

Bodhi leaf with the monk Phra Kru Suntornthammamopat depicted in the centre.

Top: A Bodhi leaf decoration with gold relief.

Above Left: A decorative Bodhi leaf on the ceiling of a Bangkok cab.

Left: Nang Gwak beckons from the centre of a bodhi leaf.

In Bangkok cabs, you occasionally encounter a real Bodhi leaf that has been dried and preserved, but most leaves are representations made out of paper. Colours range from bright blue, red, or yellow to metallic. They're typically printed or collaged with images of important monks or the Buddha and they generally include sacred text and symbols. Taxi drivers like to hang them from their rearview mirrors and sometimes they attach them to car ceilings. To keep them safe, they're normally laminated in plastic.

While Bodhi trees, and in particular Bo leaves, are popular Buddhist motifs, the earliest accounts of the Buddha's enlightenment fail to make any arboricultural references, so it's possible that the legend is a later addition to Buddhist folklore.

Bangkok taxi drivers that follow the cult of the Bodhi tree probably aren't very concerned about the history behind it anyway. Cabbies are more interested in how it potentially helps them to attract more passengers, bring in more profit, and protect them from cantankerous commuters and crazy drivers that share the same roads.

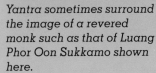

Above right: A medallion in the form of a bodhi leaf includes the image of a monk and twin stupas.

Opposite: The dried veins of a real bodhi leaf are preserved as a memento.

NEVER TOO CUTE

Fifty-year-old ladies toting Hello Kitty handbags, grown men donning t-shirts with classic American cartoon characters, and business people absorbed in manga comic books. Welcome to adulthood in Thailand. In this culture, there's no age limit for being infatuated with all things sweet, innocent, happy, huggable, and cute.

Even Bangkok cab drivers can't resist collecting whimsical accessories and other playful memorabilia to display in their taxis. The stereotype of gruff, stone-faced taxi drivers who prefer cab interiors with a single pine-scented air freshener as their only accessory doesn't usually apply in this city. Many Bangkok cabbies would rather take a more lighthearted approach to life and to their occupation. And according to some drivers, they're simply trying to create a friendly atmosphere for their passengers.

In the cabs you can find representations of action figures with spiky hair, stickers of popular cartoon characters on windows, toy Godzillas with braces on their teeth, and collectibles in the form of Doraemon, the Japanese cat-like robot figure that is supposed to be from the future. Other characters that can be spotted in Bangkok taxis range from The Incredible Hulk to Bashful from *Snow White and the Seven Dwarfs*.

Of course, you can also find many toy animals in the taxis. To name a few, there are Thai elephant trinkets, plastic pink bunnies and monkeys, as well as novelties in the form of lions, tigers, and bears, including pandas which have been all the rage here in the past few years. The craze was set off when the first giant panda was born in Thailand at the Chiang Mai Zoo. Named Lin Bing, the young panda has recently returned to its Chinese homeland but while it was here, the youngster was the subject of a nationwide

Godzilla figure with braces snarls on a Thai taxi dashboard.

*A range of emotions
depicted on the dashboard.*

craze, with hordes of Thais making pilgrimages to visit Lin Bing, and a Thai cable company launching a Panda Channel with regular updates on the celebrity animal's daily activities.

Another creature that is commonplace in Thai taxis is the infamous waving cat. Popular throughout Asia and in Chinese and Thai restaurants abroad, this puss is associated with good fortune. The character originates from Japan where she is known as Maneki Neko and is based on a real historical feline that lured a wealthy patron into a poor temple. Today, this happy cat beckons customers with one paw and usually holds a gold coin with the other to represent prosperity. Another version of this cat who sometimes appears in Bangkok cabs is known as Hello Kitty.

One classic car accoutrement that you occasionally see in Bangkok cabs is bobbleheads. Invented in the 1950s in the United States, they're sometimes known as nodders or wobblers. These tchotchkes with bouncing heads typically depict famous athletes, musicians, actors, or cartoon characters. Some of the most famous bobbleheads include representations of The Beatles, Elvis, and Baseball Hall of Famer, Willie Mays. In Thai taxis, however, animals such as dogs with wobbling heads are more popular.

*A plastic monkey and flower
add cheer to the taxi.*

In Bangkok cabs, futuristic-looking novelties and baby-faced baubles are displayed alongside images of the gods and other sacred icons. It's not uncommon to see a statuette of the Buddha, for example, surrounded by plastic posable figures. The result is a blissful conglomeration of idols that are equally idealised and worshipped.

For newcomers and visitors to Bangkok, the combinations of things in the taxis may seem funny and a bit strange. Some might even deem the practice of combining religion with pop culture blasphemous. But for the cab drivers and for most Thai people, the juxtapositions are commonplace and unremarkable.

Puppy stickers embellish a rearview mirror and a taxi meter along with an image of the Buddha.

Thais and Bangkok taxi drivers are crazy about pandas.

A pink toy bunny beside a Bangkok cabby's license.

A flying pig sticker adds whimsy to the console.

The ubiquitous lucky waving cat is thought to bring in more business.

In Thailand, rabbits appear in folktales, in sayings, in astrology, as trademarks, and of course, in some taxis.

Bobblehead pooch waggles his head as the taxi turns corners and meanders through traffic.

Two playful Doraemon figures.

A blue shark toy motorbike appears to ascend the dashboard.

Perhaps the appreciation for anything adorable is related to the Thai fascination with Japanese culture and a burgeoning interest in anything that the Japanese regard as cute, or in slang terms, *kawaii*. In Thailand, you can buy donuts in the shape of sushi, watch Japanese cartoons dubbed in Thai on TV, and get an impractical 'J-Pop' hairstyle at the salon. And in Bangkok taxis, many of the collectible characters are of Japanese origin.

In Thai culture, having fun, or *sanuk*, is a main objective in most situations, so it makes sense that most Thais enjoy anything that doesn't take itself too seriously. After all, the attainment of happiness is a major goal in Buddhism. For some, cuteness offers refuge from the reality of everyday worklife. And it's also a reminder to everyone to lighten up and not to worry about the small stuff, like getting stuck at a red light for fifteen minutes.

A motley collection of characters.

Stuffed toy creatures among taxi talismans.

Following pages: Yellow ceramic frogs, plastic penguins on skis, and a toy crab saluting the USA on a Bangkok taxi dashboard.

A typically unlikely combination of figures and characters in a Bangkok cab.

Acknowledgements

**Thank You
Khob Khun Khrub
ขอบคุณครับ**

Bangkok Taxi Drivers for inspiring me and for allowing me to photograph your talismans;

River Books for giving my book the opportunity to come to fruition. A special thank you to Narisa Chakrabongse, Paisarn Piemmettawat, and Stephen Murphy for your helpfulness and guidance;

Carol Siatras, Kiki Anderson, Didier Leplae, Amanda Proeber, Kim Miller, and Lillie for your camaraderie in Bangkok;

Kiki for composing the brilliant preface of the book;

Dynaya Bhutipunthu ('Dow'), Karen Siatras, and Tulaya Pornpitikulchai for your design expertise and creative input;

All my teachers in the past who have helped to shape my beliefs about life and art;

Colleagues, administration, and staff at Mahidol University International College for your support;

Friends far and near who share my passion for creativity;

My students over the years who have taught me as much, if not more, than what I've taught you;

Mike, Robin, Alek, Derrik, Calvin, Lizzi, Shelley, Steve, Karly, and Katie for your unconditional love and encouragement;

Dad and Kathy for your understanding and for believing in me;

Mom who always told me I can do anything if I want to badly enough.

Opposite: Two bunches of fresh orchids bless a Thai taxi.